The World's Own Book: Or The Treasury Of A Kempis

Percy Fitzgerald

THE WORLD'S OWN BOOK

OR

THE TREASURY OF À KEMPIS

An Account of the chief Editions of "The Imitation of Christ"
with an Analysis of its methods

BY

PERCY FITZGERALD M.A. F.S.A.

"The world has opened its arms to receive it"—Dr. Johnson

LONDON
ELLIOT STOCK 62 PATERNOSTER ROW E.C.

1895

THOMAS Á KEMPIS.

Photographed from the Portrait of Geertrindenberg.

CONTENTS.

———

The World's own Book or The Treasury of à Kempis.

———

Who hath not heard it spoken,
How deep you were within the Books of God?
Shakespeare.

———

CHAPTER THE FIRST.

DR. JOHNSON AND "THE IMITATION"—SHAKESPEARE—THE EDITIO PRINCEPS—ELZEVIR EDITIONS AND OTHERS.

NOT long ago, in the great Reading Room of the Museum, I had open before me a small "lean" folio of one hundred and seventy-six leaves, one of the early "Incunables" or "Fifteeners." It was bright and clean, as though it had been issued only yesterday from the press, with that air of elegance and picturesque dignity which distinguishes so many of these early efforts. It was arrayed in a handsome purple "jacket," and bore the crown and monogram of George III., to whose fine library, now known as "The King's," it belonged. It was actually the first printed issue of *The Imitation*, or *Following, of Christ*, the work of Gunther Zainer, sent forth from the good city of "Augus. Vindel," or Augsburg.

It was a strange, curious feeling, the having before one, and holding in one's hand, the parent of such a progeny—for there

B

have been more copies of the *Imitation* printed than of any book save the Bible. It is the most popular and most read. No other work written by man has enjoyed, and still enjoys, such a circulation, for, as Fontenelle has said, the Bible is not to be counted an exception, since it came from the Almighty. It would be curious and interesting to speculate how many hundred thousand souls it may have saved, or put on the way to salvation; and, by a poetical stretch, I could fancy, as I turned over the pages, that their grateful spirits were fluttering around in the air, blessing the old tome.

Dr. Johnson, describing the extraordinary favour enjoyed by this great book, used the happy phrase, "The world has opened its arms to receive it." He then quoted a passage which, he said, had always struck him forcibly. "If thou canst not make thyself such as thou wouldst be, how canst thou expect to have another exactly to thy mind?" This shows the value of criticism from such an intellect as Johnson's, which, almost without effort, always seized on what was most striking or telling. Many persons who have studied their *Imitation* may have overlooked this pregnant saying, or perhaps have not noticed its extraordinary force. They have read the book as they would any religious work of meditation, or have been attracted by other passages of a more conventional kind. Yet this truth, so irresistibly logical and convincing, when we reflect on it a moment, seems to comprise the entire rule of a religious life. A zealous person, wishing to make his neighbour better, and with an eagle-eye for blemishes, will find himself checked in his efforts as he encounters this wholesome saying: and with a sort of shame, and a smile even, will have to own, that the reforming of others ought, for decency's sake, to include the reforming of himself: and that if he be lenient to himself, others are entitled to the same indulgence. When repeating this saying to friends, I have always noted how much they are impressed, as by some novelty. It may be said, indeed, that no better specimen could be chosen to convey an idea of the general wisdom and sound common-sense of this wonderful book.

But Johnson's faith in the *Imitation* was extraordinary. On one occasion he quoted a statement that it " had been printed in one language or other as many times as there have been months since it first came out." His various editors have cried out against the exaggeration of this assertion. Malone made the calculation that this would amount to nearly four thousand editions, which he seems to dismiss as absurd. Mr. Croker adopts this view, and Dr. B. Hill wonders that Johnson did not apply "his favourite test for exaggeration, viz., counting." He implies that if Johnson had done so he would at once have seen the absurdity. The last editor, Mr. Mowbray Morris, says that he "seems to have lapsed from a distinctive mark of his character, the *incredulus odi*." But all these wise men, who are so "cock sure," are quite astray here, and it is remarkable that Johnson, who in other instances was certain to scoff such statements out of court, should here have accepted this tale with honest faith. Some thirty or forty years ago, Père Becker laboriously formed a list of all the editions, and discovered that there were at least three thousand, and when preparing a new edition of his work enrolled nearly three thousand more, thus completely substantiating Johnson's statement, with a handsome margin to boot.

À Kempis and Shakespeare may be fitly joined in company.

Indeed there is in the "Bard" a divine fulness and dignity which often suggest our author. There is the same grand reserve as in the lines placed at the beginning of these speculations:

> Who hath not heard it spoken,
> How deep you were within the Books of God?

He has innumerable passages exactly in the tone and spirit of the *Imitation.* Such as:

> Let me be ignorant and in nothing good
> But graciously to know I am no better.
>
> If thou'rt rich, thou'rt poor,
> For, like an ass whose back with ingots bows,
> Thou bear'st thy heavy riches but a journey,
> And death unloads thee.
>
> He's truly valiant, that can wisely suffer
> The worst that man can breathe, and make his wrongs
> His outsides: to wear them like his raiment carelessly
> And ne'er prefer his injuries to his heart
> To bring it into danger.
>
> You have too much respect upon the world—
> They lose it that do buy it with much care.
>
> Talkers are no good doers.
>
> We must not stint
> Our necessary actions, in the fear
> To cope malicious censures.
>
> Love thyself last: cherish those hearts that hate thee
> Still in thy right hand carry gentle peace
> To silence envious tongues: Be just and fear not.

One would surely think that he had read his *Imitation.*

There seems to be something prodigious or even miraculous, associated with this book, even at its starting, as though a portent of the course that was before it. It is thought wonderful that over a score of editions of the Holy Bible appeared between the date of the invention of printing and the close of the fifteenth century. But few would suppose how many editions of the *Imitation* came forth in that period. No less than *eighty* have been counted up, and there are likely to be more.

Boswell mentions: " I had seen in the King's library, sixty-three editions of my favourite Thomas à Kempis, amongst which it (*i.e.* one) was in eight languages: Latin, German, French, Italian, Spanish, English, and Armenian;" on which Johnson said that he thought it unnecessary to collect many editions of a book which were all the same, except as to the paper and print; "he would have the original and all the translations, and all the editions which had any variation in the text." It will be noticed that the worthy, impulsive Boswell calls it his "favourite." It is scarcely known that when a young man at college, he was actually converted to the Catholic faith, and though he was later talked out of these opinions, he was during his life, like his great chief, all but a Catholic at heart. No one, indeed, could make " a favourite book " of the *Imitation* without imbibing, through the pores, as it were, a genuine Catholic feeling. Which suggests the well-meant, but rather laboured, attempts of Protestant admirers to force it into some sort of harmony with their opinions, or at least to neutralize and render colourless the more "awkward" portions. This would seem a desperate undertaking. Some have indeed "cut the claws," and boldly suppressed what was too plainly expressed. It may be said, however, that no Protestant can honestly read or admire the book, without being confronted with this inconsistency.

Returning to the small lean folio that I held in my hands at the Museum, it seems to have been thought so lightly of, that it was sent out as one among a collection of pious treatises, such as "*Hieronimus et Gennadius de viris illustribus : Idem de essentiâ divinitatis : Thomas Aquinas de articulis fidei : Augustinus de quantitate animi : idem de soliloquio : Speculum peccatoris :*" &c. Then after these came, modestly introduced, "Libri iv. *De Imitatione Christi,*" running to seventy-six folios. Four other treatises follow. But this little treatise is the only one of the collection that has the printer's name at the end. It seems therefore likely that it was at first issued separately, and was later joined to the other treatises.

It might be interesting to recall the names of the spirited, venturous printers who were the first to introduce great books to the world : such as the Kobergers and others, who issued the Bible ; Isaac Jaggard and his partner, who gave us Shakespeare ; Constable, who brought out the Waverley Novels ; Moxon, to whom we owe *Elia;* the publishers of *Don Quixote*, of *Robinson Crusoe*, of *Gulliver's Travels*, and of the *Vicar of Wakefield*, and many more. The name of the worthy Gunther or Ginther Zainer, the first publisher of the *Imitation*, deserves on this account to be enshrined in all hearts. He thus introduces the work : "*Viri egregii Thomœ montis S. Agnetis in Trajecto regularis canonici Libri de Xti Imitatione numero quatuor finiunt feliciter per Gintheum Zainer ex Reutlingen progenitum litteris impssi ahenis Augustœ-Vindel.*"

That is to say : "The four Books on the Imitation of Christ, by that eminent man Thomas, Canon Regular of Mount St. Agnes, in Utrecht, happily finished by Ginther Zainer, born at Reutlingen, and printed from bronze type at Augsburg."

Fili ego debeo ee finis tuus supmus z vltimate
si ve desideras esse beatus Ex hac intencoe pur-
gabitur affectus tuus sepius ad seipsum et ad
creaturas male curatus Nã si teipm in aliquo qris
stati in te deficis et arescis. Oia ergo ad me principa-
liter referas qz ego sũ qui oia tibi Sic singula cõsidera
sicut ex summo bono manantia. Nam ad me tanqã
ad suũ originem cũcta ẽẽ reducenda. Ex me pusillus
et magnus. paup et diues tanqã ex fonte viuo aquã
hauriunt viuã Et qui mihi sponte et libere deseruiũt-
gram pro gra accipient. Qui aũt extra me voluerit
gliari vel in aliq priuato bono delectari nõ stabilietur
impedietur et angustiabitur Nihil ergo tibi de bono
ascribere debes nec alicui homi virtutem attribuas. ʃ
totũ est a deo sine q nihil habet homo Ego totũ dedi
ego totũ rehabere volo. et cũ magna districtõe grãr
actões requiro Hec est veritas q fugatur glie vanitas.
Et si intrauerit celestis glia et vera caritas. non erit
aliqua inuidia. nec contractio cordis. neqz priuatus
amor occupabit Vincit. n. omnia diuina caritas et
dilatat omes aie vires Si recte sapis in me solo gau-
debis. in me solo spabis. qz nemo bonꝰ nisi solus deꝰ
qui est sup oia laudandus et benedicendus in omnibꝰ
              Qz spreto mundo dulce est seruire deo   Cap. xi.
Nunc iterz loquor domine et non silebo. dicaz
in auribꝰ dei mei et regis mei q est in excelso
O qm magna mltitudo dulcedinis tue quã
abscondisti timentibꝰ te Deꝰ qd es amantibꝰ. quid
toto corde tibi seruientibus Vere ineffabilis dulcedo
cõtemplacõis tue quam largiris amantibꝰ te In hoc
maxime ostendisti mihi dulcedinem caritatis tue. qz
cum non essem fecisti me. et cum errarem longe a te
reduxisti me vt seruirem tibi. et precepisti michi vt
diligam te O fons amoris perpetui quid dicam de te
quomodo potero tui obliuisci. qui me dignatus es

*Reduced facsimile page of the first edition of " The Imita-
tion of Christ," printed at Augsburg, 1471-72.*

He supplies no date; but the year is either 1470 or 1471. Bibliographers can fix dates very accurately from the form of the letters used and the general character of the printing. It is pleasant, therefore, to think that the excellent author, who died in 1472, may have just lived to see the first printed copy of his invaluable treatise. Zainer ventures on the amiable boast that he has printed it "with the utmost accuracy" (*accuratissime*). A learned bibliographer, Baron Weestreenen, contends that this calling attention to the type, "*literis ahenis*," means that it was stereotyped, which is surely pushing the thing too far. The printer was merely claiming credit for using bronze letters, instead of, I suppose, the usual lead ones.

But now follows a curious and rather perplexing thing. Shortly after à Kempis' death in 1472, there appeared a collection of his works in one tome, a pretty quarto of the usual small size, and brightly printed, but which does not contain the *Imitation*! This, no doubt, is a great point for the Gersonites. For it was published at Utrecht, not far away from Mount St. Agnes. The publishers were Ketelaer and G. de Keempt.

One of the most interesting of the early editions is that issued from Nuremburg in the year 1494. It is remarkable from the controversial nature of the title, which ran: "*Opera et libri vite fratris Thomæ de Kempis ordinis canonicorum regularium, quorum titulos vide in primo folio Andreæ Assti Anno Christi 1494. Nurembergie per Caspar Hochfeder.*" It contained 182 pages in double column, each column having fifty-three lines. And it sets forth this rather exceptional claim, in a form rarely found in books of the period: "*Dulcissimi ac Divi Thome de Kempis . . . de Imitatione Xti opus: qd falso apud Vulgares Gersoni Parisiensi cancellario impingit . . . libell. prm. incipit.*"

This very significant utterance shows that a hot controversy was already being carried on as to the authorship; the terms "most sweet and heavenly," applied to the writer, suggest the devotion of partisanship. The words "falsely credited by the vulgar" are rather unusual in books of the time.

The worthy printer, Caspar Hochfeder, at the close of the book, modestly claims credit for the pains and care with which it had been printed.[1] It contains various other works of the author, in what is called German text, set out with all kinds of puzzling abbreviations; but the *Imitation* is placed first, an evidence of its importance. There is also found here a curious letter prefixed, addressed by a Carthusian, Father Kechhamer, to "Master Peter Danhauser," in which he reminds the latter of his former devotion to books of poetry and philosophy, with some hints of his neglect of spiritual things; and he invites him to atone for his neglect by careful study of these writings, and by editing and seeing through the press this admirable book. "Master Peter," acknowledging his former laxity, engages to give his best care and pains to the task. At the end it is styled "a golden treatise, and exceeding useful, on the perfect imitation of Christ and the true contempt of the world."

There is an edition without date or place (*sine anno et*

---

[1] This claim shows how well the work, though unpublished, had come to be known during the fifty years since it was written. The number of MS. copies which are now in existence—in England alone there are nearly a score—shows that it enjoyed a "large circulation." Some of these are in the handwriting of the author, who was a great and skilful copyist, and had copied the whole Scriptures in three or four years. My friend, Dr. Inglis, who has a rare and choice library of "cradle works," possesses a sort of practice book, that once belonged to one of the illuminators. It is full of experiments, unfinished initial letters, and the like. On one page we find "the alphabet of Thomas à Kempis, the monk," a number of pious sayings commencing "A, B, or C," &c., to the last letter. The owner is inclined to think it is the work of à Kempis himself.

loco, description dear to the bibliographers), with a curious reference in the title, which supports the contention that the name of the work was accidentally taken from the first chapter. It runs: "*Libellus consolatorius ad instructionem devotorum, cujus primum capitulum est de imitatione Christi et contemptu omnium vanitatum mundi. Et quidam totum libellum sic appellant scilicet libellum de imitatione Christ.*" That is: " A little book for the instruction of the devout, whose first chapter is on the Imitation of Christ and the contempt of all the vanities of the world. And there are certain who thus style the whole book, to wit, 'The Book of the Imitation of Christ.'" In one early edition without date, we even find the three claimant authors in company: to wit, Thomas à Kempis, Gerson, and St. Bernard. "*Tractatus fratris Thome de Kempis canonici regularis ordinis: St. Augustini de Imitatione Christi, &c., cum tractaculo Gerson de meditatione cordis: Speculum Bernardi de vita.*"

The publishers often became so intrigued by these claims of authorship, that we find them at times passing by the matter altogether. One simply announced that it was by "*quodam viro religioso;*" another gave merely the title of the book as: "*Incipiunt ammonicones ad spiritualem vitam utiles. Cap. primum de imitacoe Xpi. In civit Meteui Colini 1482.*" But only the first book is given. An edition of 1485 announces it to be the work of "Gerson *Cangelarii*" (*sic*): another calls him "Maistre *Jarson.*" Bibliographers note that the first edition, with a date, that claims Gerson as the author, is that of 1485.

Every one has heard of the Elzevirs, whose elegant little "pocket" volumes, printed with exquisite taste, used to be the delight of collectors. About the middle of the seventeenth

century they issued their edition, which is still considered the
most rare, charming, and costly of the series.   The Elzevirs
were the great Protestant printing house of Amsterdam and
Leyden: while the Plantins—whose enticing workshops are
still shown at Antwerp—issued a Catholic edition. People often
smile at the enthusiasm displayed over these and other typographical "curios," but such is unreasoning and unreasonable
prejudice.   This book, in particular, is a beautiful and elegant
thing, from the smooth "satiny" paper, the exquisite outlines of
the lettering, and the picturesque harmony of the page.   It is
closely printed: yet the effect is most clear and distinct.   It
was even said that they used silver type: but it is likely to have
been bronze, to secure clearness and sharpness.   An Elzevir
à Kempis in fine condition—a tall copy is measured in milli-
metres—fetches three, four, and even five pounds.   You must
see, too, that you have the right issue, for there were three of
this one edition.[1]

[1] In one of their rare little classics—the genuine edition, like and equal to the
others in every point save one—you must take care that you find "the Bull's
Head" somewhere, or you are undone.

*Title-page of the Elzevir edition of " The
Imitation of Christ."*

CHAPTER THE SECOND.

T is gratifying to find that two of our most famous English printers, Wynkyn de Worde and Pynson, were the first to print the *Imitation* in English. But it seems strange that Caxton, who printed so many devotional works, should not have thought of introducing the *Imitation* to his countrymen. Wynkyn de Worde's edition is without date, and is thus described: "*A* full *deuoute and gosteley Treatyse of ye* Imytaciō *and* Followynge *ye blessyd Lyfe* of our Mercifull Saviour Cryst. The same compyled in Latin by the right worshipfull Doctor Mayster John Gerson: translated into English in the year of our Lorde MDII. by Mayster Wyllyam at Kynson Doctor of Dyvynte, at the special request and commandment of the full excellent Pryncesse Margate Moder to our Soveraigne Lord Kynge Henry the VII. and Comtesse of Rychemont and Dudley." This pious lady, by the way, had already interested herself in one of Caxton's ventures. In 1490, that printer had issued "*The Fifteen O's, and other Prayers,* printed by commandment of the Princess Elizabeth, and also of the Princess Margaret, by their most humble subject and servant, William Caxton."

The translation of the Fourth Book, on the Holy Eucharist,

was the work of the Princess herself, and the whole is garnished with the arms of the King, and those of the royal translator. The title sets forth: "Here beginneth the forthe Boke of ye followynge Jesu Cryst and of the Contempnynge of the World. In prynted at the Commandment of the most excelent Princess Margaret and by the same Pryncess it was translate out of Frenche into Englysshe in fourme and maner aforesaide the yere of Lorde our God MDII." The translation is quaint enough and effective. It commences with what it styles a "Prologue." "Come to Me, seythe our mercyfull Lord, all tht laboreth *and be charged*, and I shall give unto you Refeccyon." "Be charged" is pleadingly forcible.

A specimen of the translation, taken from the earlier "Bokes," will be found interesting.

"Oh! how jocund and pleasant a life should it be to a soul, that had no worldly thing to do but love God continually, with all his heart, in works and words! Oh! if we might continue in this life without bodily refection, as eating and drinking, sleeping or any other bodily refection of our soul; then we should be much more happy than we be now, in serving and attending more for bodily things than ghostly profit. When man cometh once to that perfection, that he seeketh consolation of no creature, then beginneth he to have a spiritual *tallage* in God: and when he is content with every fortune, as well with adversity as prosperity: confirming and referring all his words to God to serve and to obey His will. Ever remember the end of everything that thou beginnest; and also, that, time lost cannot be recovered: and thou shalt never obtain virtue without labour and diligence: and when thou beginnest to be remiss in spiritual labours then thou beginnest to wax evil."

feruent & louynge foule is euer redy to all thynges
þ be expedyēt to the plefure of god & fpirytuall pro-
fite of it felfe. It is moze labour to refyft byce and in
ozdinate paffions/than to be occuppied in bodely labours and if þ wylt not gyue hede to auoyde þ leffe
fynne thou fhalte foone be enduced to the moze. And
whan thou haft bzought the day to the euyntyde in
ftuous occupacion without ony grete difplefure to
our lozde than thou mayft be glad & furely take thy
reft in hym. And euer befoze all other foules take he
de to thyn owne foule excpte & moue thy felfe to ftu
and what fo euer thou doeft be neuer neclygente in
thofe thynges that be neceffary foz the foule & loke
how moche thou defyzeft to pfite/& fo moche aplye
thy felfe byolently to gooftly & fpyzytuall labours.
And thus endeth the fyzfte boke of Johñ Gerfon of
the Imitacion of Chzyft.

¶Here begynneth the .ij. boke of Johñ Gerz
fon of the inwarde & deuoute conuerfacyon of
the foule of man.

After the fentence of our fauyour Jefu
Cryfte the inwarde regne of god is in
foule of man. Retourne thy felfe with
all thy herte to oure lozde and fozfake
the inozdynate loue of the wozlde and
thy foule fhall fynde reft / lerne to con-
tempne outwarde thynges & apply thy mynde to
inwarde thynges and thou fhalt perceyue that the

Facsimile page of the first English Edition of "The Imitation of Christ."

Nor was this the only English royal personage associated with the book. Catherine Parr, the Queen, or one of the Queens, of Henry VIII., prepared a little volume of *Prayers and Meditations*, drawn from the *Imitation* itself.

Another famous English printer, Pynson, also supplied an edition: "The Imytacion and Followynge of Christ Emprynted in London by Rycharde Pynson. The yere of our Lorde MDIII the XXVII day of June. At the George Flete Strete." This was a duodecimo, and was virtually Wykyn's version altered and amended. Our printer, however, cannot refrain from "vilipending" a little his predecessor's work. "And though III. of the first Bokes have been before this tyme right well and devoutly translated into Englysshe by a famous Clerke called Maister Wyllyam Atkinson which was a Doctour of Divinitie yet for as moche as the sayd translator for some cause hym moving in divers places lifte out moche parte of some of the chapytres, and some varied fro the letter—therefore the said III. Bokes be eftomes translatyd." It is then objected to the Princess' translation of the Fourth Book that it was done out of the French and therefore "could not follow the Latyn *so nighe*." Princess Margaret and her pious work was thus treated pretty much as she might have been by a modern reviewer. It is remarkable that, both in England and in France, the book should have thus been stamped by royal patronage.

It is creditable to devout Protestant appreciation of the *Imitation* that the first Protestant translation should have been made so early as the year 1580. It is often supposed that Stanhope's was the first; at least this is the version most generally found in libraries, or "on the stalls." This rare edition is thus described: "Kempis (Thomas à).—*Of the*

Imitation of Christ, Three, both for Wisdome and Godliness, most excellent Books, made 170 yeeres since by One Thomas of Kempis, and for the Worthiness thereof oft since translated out of Latin into Sundrie Languages, by divers godlie and learned men, Now newlie corrected, translated, and with most ample textes of the Holie Scriptures illustrated by Thomas Rogers. Imprinted at London by Henry Denham, dwelling in Paternoster Row, at the signe of the Starre, being the assigne of William Seres 1580." "Woodcut frontispiece, engraving on reverse of last page of Preface, and printer's colophon at end of book, 12mo, A very large copy in old sheep, with many rough leaves, genuine and unwashed throughout. This," adds Messrs. Pickering, "the First Edition of Rogers' Version, we believe to be almost unique, it being hitherto undescribed ; the earliest edition quoted by Watt, Lowndes, Allibone, and other Bibliographers, is that of four years later (1584)." The price asked for this rarity was £10. Another early version was that of John Worthington made in 1677. Here is a quaint description of another of the English versions : "A boke newly translated out of Latyn into Englysshe called *The Followynge of Chryste.* Hereafter followethe a boke called in Latyn *Imitatio Christis,* that is to say in Englissh, *The Followynge of Christe,* wheren be contand four lytell Bokes, which boke, as some men affairme was first made and compyled in Latyn by the famous clerke Mayster Johnan Gern." This *Followynge of Christe* has always been a favourite title, though as a translation of *Imitatio* it is scarcely warranted. "Following" is less strict, has more independence than "Imitation."

But there have been innumerable versions in English, Catholic and Protestant. A favourite title was *The Christian*

Pattern. Stanhope's version has a certain archaic flavour which corresponds with the text.   But not unnaturally the plain Catholic doctrine, exhibited in passages dealing with the Eucharist, led to some very serious alterations of the text. I say, not unnaturally, because the position was an embarrassing one.

That worthy bibliomaniac, Dr. T. Frognal Dibdin, also furnished a translation, with an Introduction and Portrait, which was issued by Pickering in 1828.   It need not be said it is worthy of the translator's taste in typography.   "A'Kempis. —*Of the Imitation of Christ*, translated from the Latin, with a long and valuable historical and literary Introduction by T. F. Dibdin ; *illustrated with a portrait of A'Kempis, a beautiful portrait of Christ after Guercino, an engraving of Da Vinci's Last Supper, and 3 other plates, all engraved on copper in the most finished manner.   Pickering and Major, 1828."*

A notable edition was that of Sebastian Castalio, who had edited the Bible, and who gave an edition "in elegant Latin, reprinted here and abroad, and often put into the hands of our youth at Cambridge."   This amounted to rewriting the work, a rather "free and easy" proceeding.

The fashion in which the work was re-fashioned in the English translations, or rather adaptations, could not be better illustrated than by the following : " *The Christian Pattern, or, The Imitation of Jesus Christ*, being the genuine Works of Thomas à Kempis, containing Four Books, viz. : 1. The sigh of a penitent soul, or, a treatise of true compunction. 2. A short Christian Directory.   3. Of Spiritual Exercises. 4. Of Spiritual Exercises, or, the Soliloquy of the Soul.   Translated from the original Latin, *and recommended by George Hicks, LL.D.*   1707."

This last item is "good." To conceive of this great work of all the world being patronizingly "recommended" by one "George Hicks, LL.D."!

Another of these "adaptations" was issued in 1841, in which all the "awkward" passages were taken out, and consigned to notes at the end ; and to the work is given this praise, that it can be satisfactorily "compared with the *Sacra Privata*" of Bishop Wilson, a work of which the world in general does not know so much as it does of the *Imitation.* The Bishop however thought, it seems, that "in order to dispose our hearts to devotion, the active life is to be preferred to the contemplative." "Doubtless," the editor adds, "to both of these holy men may not inaptly be applied the words of the poet :

> Self have I worn out thrice thirty years,
> Some in much joy, and many in tears,
> Yet never complained of cold or heat,
> Of summer's flame, nor of winter's threat,
> He never was to fortune foeman,
> But gently took that urgently came,
> And ever my flock was my chief care,
> Winter and summer they mought well fare."

Which is almost ludicrously inapplicable, at least to Thomas à Kempis, who was not likely to give a thought to "summer's flame or winter's threat," or to think of fortune as "a foeman," and had no "flock" to look after. But it shows how almost unintelligible is the real Catholic principle to those outside. The translation, which is one of 1677, is moreover very bald, and suggests an attempt to copy the forms of the Book of Common Prayer. Witness the opening verses : "These are the words of Christ by which we are admonished how we ought to imitate His life and manners, if we will be truly enlightened, &c. Let therefore our chiefest endeavour be, to meditate upon the life of Christ. The doctrine of Christ exceedeth all the doctrines of holy men," &c.

In 1889 another odd but well-meant version was attempted in England, under Ritualistic inspiration, in the shape of an English translation "now for the first time set forth in rhythmic sentences, according to the original intention of the author." It was garnished with a Preface, the work of the late Canon Liddon, and has reached a second edition. This is of course founded on the musical theories of the German Hirsche, which seem a little fantastic and far-fetched. He fancied he had discovered in the original MS. various cabalistic marks addressed to the reader, which seemed to direct that a metrical form should be given to the recitation. But I suspect this is quite accidental, and after the principle of the " Shakon-Bakespeare" controversy. It will be recalled that there are passages in the *Old Curiosity Shop* which take this metrical shape in a very curious way. Dickens, however, certainly never intended such a thing. There was yet another Protestant, or High Church translation in our own time by Mr. Keble. And Mr. Elliot Stock—*himself Kempisissimus*—has just issued, too, an exact *fac simile* of the first edition, with an introductory essay by another High Churchman, Canon Knox Little. I have been assured that it is the fashion among Protestants of a more robust type to prefer Bogatzy's *Golden Treasury*, which is considered a treatise of much the same character and merit.

The favourite Catholic translation was issued in 1744, and was the work of Dr. Challoner, whose well-known initials, " R. C.," are attached to it. This, I presume, is the popular

C

version now in use.   It was fortunate that it was attempted
thus early, though scarcely early enough, for it is cast in
a rather antique and quaint phraseology.   Our modern familiar
tongue could never suitably present the author's ideas.[1]

In all there have been the astounding number of some sixty
translations into French of the great book.   The French *editio
princeps* is ushered in thus quaintly: "*Cy comance le liure
tressalutaire de la ymitacio Jhesu Christ e mesprisement de ce
monde, premiermet compose en Latin par saint bernard ou par
autre deuote persone attribue a maistre jehan Gerson. . . . et apres
translate en francoys en la cite de Tholouse. . . . Cy finist le liure
de le ymitacion. . . . imprime a Tholose par maistre henric Mayer
alaman lan de grace mil. ccc. LXXXVIII. et le XXVIII. jour de
May.*"   This, like all very early French "cradle" works, is of
extraordinary rarity, and it was not until the year 1812 that the
Royal Library at Paris was able to secure a copy.   In most of
the early French editions we find the work styled *tressalutaire.*
This title is almost amusing from the very cautious speculation
exhibited.   The reader may take his choice of St. Bernard or of
" some other pious person," though it " has been attributed to
Maistre Jehan Gerson."

The Italian issue, oddly enough, was of the same year :
"*Giovanni Gerson dell' imitation di Christo e del dispregio del
mondo venezia Rosso de vercelle 1488.*"   The German was earlier
than either, by two years.   We find "*Ein ware nachuolgung
Christi Augspurg, Ansorg. 1486.*"

One of the most gratifying instances of the compelling

---

[1] I find in a catalogue this tribute to the influence of the author : " A'Kempis :
Of the Imitation of Christ.   Translated by F. P. Bamfylde.   A neatly written
MS. for the use of his two daughters Bridget and Mary, 12mo, calf, 15s."

power, or magic even of the *Imitation,* is the great Corneille's association with it. On his plays being received with some coldness he turned his thoughts and energies to the translation of the great book. According to another story this was imposed on him by his confessor as a penance. The poet, however, entered on his task *con amore;* it was a business of extraordinary difficulty and drudgery, but he continued to translate not the *Imitation* merely, but Psalms, Offices, &c., often reverting to his *Imitation,* whence he drew meditations and reflections, which he cast into metrical shape. Here are some specimens of his translation :

Qui ergo se abstrahabit a notis et amicis, approximabit ille Deus cum angelis sanctis.

> Qui se detache donc pour cette solitude
> De toutes amitiès et de toute habitude,
> Plus il rompt les liens du sang et de la chair,
> Plus de Dieu la bonté supreme,
> Par ses images et par lui meme,
> Pour le combler de biens daigne s'en approcher.

Sed humanum est, hujusmodi imaginationibus illudi :
Et parvi adhuc animi signum, tam leviter trahi ad suggestionem inimici.

> Mais l'homme de soi-meme a ces désadvantages
> Qu'il se laisse eblouir pas de vaines images ;
> Et qu'il s'en fait souvent un fantôme trompeur
> Qui tire tout à lui son espoir et sa peur.

One or two of his comments show a rare understanding of the principles of the *Imitation.* Thus he says of the author, that " having given an abundance of admirable precepts in the first two books, and wishing to ascend yet higher in the others,

and teach us the whole practice of pure spirituality, he seemed
to begin to mistrust himself : and fearful that his authority
would not carry weight enough to transport us into feelings so
detached and apart from nature, he descended from our
Saviour's seat, and introduced Him in his place." It is thus he
explains the change of style in the different books. And again :
" This grand personage (the author) has taken as much pains
not to be known, as the world has to discover him. I fancy he
would not give us the fine precept of humility *ama nesciri*, if he
had not practised it himself."

It must be said that Corneille's carries the art of dilution
and paraphrase to an extreme length, and suggests our own
Sternhold and Hopkins, or even Tate and Brady. It must be
a curious order of mind, and eminently French, that could
prefer such amplitudes to the close, nervous simplicity of the
original. He began with the experiment of a score of chapters,
but the success was so extraordinary—twenty or thirty editions
being disposed of—that he was encouraged to go on, and com-
pleted his task to the same measure of approval. So true is it,
as some one finely said, that "our good God never shows Himself
ungrateful to those who work for Him." Corneille issued a noble
edition with a scriptural engraving for every chapter. We owe
to him, too, an admirable descriptive phrase, when he calls
à Kempis " The Sovereign Author."

There was a popular French translation, first issued in
1673, by one Cusson, who besides being a publisher, was also
" an advocate of Parliament." It had an engraved *vignette* at
the head of each chapter. His son added some "reflections
and prayers" at the end of each chapter, which were written by
Father Gonnelieu, a Jesuit, and which are sound and useful

reading, though a little suggestive of the process of "painting the lily."

With one French version there is an odd story associated· The Abbé de Choisy, in 1692, issued a translation in duodecimo, with a dedication to Madame de Maintenon; one of the vignettes exhibited a lady on her knees, with a number of young girls grouped round on steps, and the motto, *Audi Filia.* The scene was naturally supposed to refer to the school of St. Cyr. The malicious wits, however, supplied the rest of the verse, *et concupiscet Rex decorem tuum.* The Abbé, who was much rallied on this account, suppressed the picture and substituted another, but in a later edition the old plate found its way back again. Nothing was sacred—even the *Imitation* itself —for "the sappers" of the Court.

CHAPTER THE THIRD.

EW books, save perhaps our own Shakespeare, have been so "glorified" in the way of what have been called "Editions of luxury." A typographical tribute to the *Imitation* was paid by King Louis XIV., who issued a quarto with a grand amplitude of page and type — the latter of such a size that each page contained only seventeen lines. A fine copy, bound in scarlet morocco, richly "tooled" and decorated with the royal arms—intended, no doubt, as a present—now lying open before me, is one of my favourite treasures. It came from the choice Osterley Park Library, to which it did honour. There is a symbolical engraving, exhibiting the glories of the Cross. This was the first work issued from the Royal Press, recently established by Cardinal Richelieu, and is a grand specimen of printing, though somewhat over "spaced." As an extraordinary contrast, I put beside it the tiniest edition known, published at Tournay in 1869. This little curio is but two inches by one and a half—and was given me by a Protestant friend. It contains 500 leaves of the thinnest and finest paper, but it weighs only a couple of ounces! The print is smaller than "diamond," yet is perfectly clear, and can be read with ease and without fatigue for at least a few pages.

I find that from this Royal Press there was also issued, in 1657, "by order of the Duke de Richelieu," a "diamond" edition of the *Imitation* "minutissimis characteribus," in company with diamond editions of *The Spiritual Combat* and the Scriptures.

Pickering also issued a diamond edition; but the first is much smaller. A huge edition was issued from Didot's Press in 1833. It professed to be based on the Arona MS. and reproduced its peculiar orthography. In 1789, the year of the Revolution, the same great firm brought out an edition—a finely printed *in-folio*. These attempts, however, paled before a wonderfully sumptuous effort made in 1854, when, to commemorate the Exhibition of that year, the Empire Press prepared a superb volume, which won all suffrages for the beauty of the type and the miniatures wrought in gold and colours, by which it was adorned. The text chosen was Corneille's metrical version. Three well-known artists were engaged in the work. Only one hundred and three copies were printed, of which the Emperor reserved seventy for himself to give away as presents. The balance of thirty was secured by a bookseller, one Masson, who charged for them a fancy price. As may be conceived, it is *rarissimus*—indeed, not to be obtained at all.

Another great printer who glorified the *Imitation* at his press was Bodoni of Parma, who issued in 1793 a superb folio, in that large, noble, spreading page, which is a note of his style. It is objected, however, that the text is inferior, being founded on the so-called "mutilated" or *tronquèd* one of Valart. He printed four special copies, each with a dedication to a royal personage, to wit: the King and Queen of Spain; the Grand

Duke of Tuscany; and the Arch-Duchess of Milan.   There were only 162 copies "taken off," fifteen of which were on "vellum paper;" so, as may be conceived, the work is rare enough.

In 1858, another French publisher, Curmer, issued an edition also splendidly illustrated, with miniatures; each page being framed in gold and colours.   The price was £6.   It must be said that the good old monk looks strange enough when decked out in these gauds.   His sound and simple Scriptural sentiments are quite out of keeping with such "flashy" adornments.   In fact, a book of this kind, which is purely didactic and reflective, cannot lend itself to illustrations which have a forced or theatrical air being dragged in, as it were, by head and shoulders.   There is no *àpropos.*

One of the most extraordinary things is the odd miscellany of persons who are associated with the book.   All sorts and conditions of intellect are found in strange fellowship.   Who could think that Renan had taken part in the discussions?   His theory was characteristic.   He put the book as far back as the thirteenth century, and supposed that it was written by an Italian.   There is another theory, to the effect that it had originally a sort of legendary or "impersonal" shape, and did not belong to any country in particular; that it dated from the middle ages, and gradually grew and developed until it assumed its present form.   Michelet and Keble, La Mennais and Ampère, Canon Liddon, Fontenelle and Renan, make an oddly-assorted company.   The Rev. Mr. Kettlewell has perhaps written what is the most scientific and scholarly work, though marked with prejudices, pardonable enough when compared with his genuine and enthusiastic appreciation of the work.

The work has always been popular in Germany, being specially adapted to German thought, and where it is said to be as much read by Protestants as by Catholics. Comte the philosopher, who used to read a chapter every day, and every day discovered new beauties hitherto hidden, attempted to explain this universal acceptance, according to his lights : "Regarded from the theoretic as distinguished from the devotional side, it throws much light on the constitution of our nature." He adds that the greater part of its practical teaching is independent of theological ideas, and that the language of the book admits of easy modification which will enable persons not accepting those ideas to use the book for self-culture. This convenient opportunist theory is plausible, but can only be accepted at the sacrifice of the sincerity of the author. It is plain that the basis of the work is doctrinal, and that those who relish merely the neutral passages must set aside or shut their eyes to the general teachings of the author. At the same time, Comte's praise of it being a contribution to the knowledge of human character, is a real compliment from such a philosopher.

Many an ardent collector has attempted to gather together all the known editions in all languages. The late Prince Lucien Bonaparte, who was so remarkable for his knowledge of tongues and dialects, possessed a vast number of copies, not surprising as a collection of editions, but each was in a different languáge, some of the most "outlandish" and unexpected kind. They were all finely bound in rich crimson morocco and gold.

Hirsche, the German writer before alluded to, issued a curious critical study of the *Imitation*, in which he proves, or tries to prove, that the system of arrangement adopted by Sommelius and others — the disposition into chapters and

paragraphs—has in many places distorted the sense. He has
made a strict collation of the original text, which, he says, has
been sorely "lacerated," rather than arranged, by this system.
There is much truth in this.   I could indeed fancy that nothing
would be more interesting than a serious, thoroughly searching
criticism, after the manner of the Shakespearian doctors, into
the fashion in which the text has been dealt with. This ought
not to be a very difficult task.   The first editor of the *Imitation*
was a Jesuit, Father Henry Sommelius, who nearly thirty years
after its first publication, took the book in hand for the purpose
of regularly "editing" it. He collated and corrected it, distributed each chapter into verses, on the model of the Scriptures.
Another Jesuit, Father Rosweyd, undertook a more critical
edition, and made a collation with the original text, to which
his is said to have most nearly corresponded.   In this form the
work passed through many editions, and seems to have been
accepted as a sort of standard one. Thus the Society is
handsomely associated with the book.

But this casting the whole into the form of paragraphs,
each purporting to be complete and finished in sense, seems
rather arbitrary.   Such necessarily gives the notion of the work
being a collection of sayings or apothegms, which is certainly
not its real character, as the sentences in many cases " run on,"
and the sense is carried forward to the succeeding ones.   The
system must do some violence to the meaning, especially when
the paragraphs are connected by conjunctions or prepositions.
Witness this specimen, where I have joined the sentences :
"Nothing is more acceptable to God, nothing more salutary for
those in this world, than to suffer willingly for Christ.   And
if thou couldst make choice thou oughtest to prefer to suffer

adversities for Christ, than be delighted with much consolation ; because thou then wouldst more resemble Christ, and be more likened to all the saints. For our merit, and the advancement of our state, consists not in having many sweetnesses and con- solations, but rather in bearing great afflictions and tribulations. If indeed there had been anything better and more beneficial to man's salvation than suffering, Christ certainly would have showed it by word and example. For He manifestly exhorts . . . all to follow Him, &c. So that when we have read," &c. All which seems to flow on consecutively.

As we have seen, Father Sommelius, in 1599, one of the early editors, was the first to cast the chapters into the form of paragraphs, each dealing with a topic. Later each paragraph was subdivided into versicles. Velart arranged sentences according to the sense. It will be interesting to give a specimen of the two systems side by side.

Here is the common version: " Son, patience and humility under adversity please me more than much devotion in prosperity.

"Why art thou afflicted at a little matter said against thee?

"If it had been more, thou oughtest not to have been disturbed.

"But now let it pass ; it is not the first, or anything new."

The other runs: " Son, patience and humility under adversity please me more than much consolation and devotion in prosperity. Why art thou afflicted at a little matter said against thee? If it had been more, thou oughtest not to have been disturbed. But now let it pass.

" It is not the first, nor anything new."

We are inclined to shrink from the tremendous controversy

of Gerson *v.* à Kempis, which has been carried on for centuries There are excellent arguments offered on both sides, and a laborious bibliophile has made a sort of list of the works written by the combatants on both sides. It seems a never-ending business. But this at least may be urged : that the general *feeling* of the world has settled that à Kempis was the writer. Further, Gerson was a professed theologian, and a voluminous writer on dogmatic and other theology ; whereas à Kempis was a devout moralist, and his book has many warnings against the dangers of theological learning, and its tendency to "puff up" or divert from the practical part of religious life.

CHAPTER THE FOURTH.

THE ORIGINAL MS. OF "THE IMITATION"—THE AUTHOR'S REAL NAME—
"DE MUSICA ECCLESIASTICÂ."

HAVE had three friends all eagerly devoted to this very fascinating subject: the late Edmund Waterton, who had sound antiquarian instincts, and in some matters was "a dungeon of research"—witness his painstaking collection on the shrines of the Blessed Virgin; Dr. Cruise, an eminent physician of Dublin; and Dr. Kells Ingram, a learned Fellow of Trinity College, Dublin. Not long before his death Edmund Waterton took up the matter with great ardour, and as a preparation had collected, I believe, over a thousand editions of the work—a very necessary and indispensable preparation, because many of the editions have prefaces and commentaries that contain much curious information. His course was unhappily cut short before he could set regularly to work, but his materials came into the hands of Mr. Wheatley, brother to the latest editor of *Pepys' Diary*, who has formed out of them an interesting work, *The Story of the Imitation.* Dr. Cruise made a pious pilgrimage to Zwolle in Holland, the burial-place of à Kempis, where some odd incidents occurred. A little box was brought to him from the sacristy, which contained the remains of the great writer, and, as the key could not be found

it was broken open *sans façon*. He was even allowed to handle
the skull and bones, which were " taken care of " in this uncere-
monious style. It is strange indeed that the relics of this holy
man, and the author of so great a book, should be " knocked
about " in this fashion. One would have thought that a decent
monument could be provided.[1]

It is known that the order of the Books as now arranged
is not the original one found in Thomas' own MS. There the
fourth, on the Eucharist, comes after the second. The third,
it is also said, was intended to be a separate work. This arrangement is supported by the fact that the third Book differs from
the others, in form, treatment, and even spirit. It is equal in
bulk to the other three Books put together. But what is very
much in favour of the theory is that the fourth Book breaks
off abruptly with, " If the works of God were such that they
could easily be comprehended by human reason, they could
neither be called wonderful nor unspeakable ;" whereas the third
Book ends with a fine inspiring prayer, a winding up, as it
were, of the whole, and concludes : " Protect and preserve
the soul of Thy poor servant amid so many dangers of this
corruptible life, and direct him by Thy accompanying grace,
along the path of peace to Thy everlasting light. Amen ! "
This is a regular *finale*.

Some years ago the publisher of these comments, Mr. Stock,
issued a *fac simile* of the original writing in a charming little
volume. The original is, it seems, preserved in the Royal Library
at Brussels. Some notes on the fly-leaf give the history of the

---

[1] Many years ago, when Swift's remains were disinterred at St. Patrick's Cathedral,
the skull was handed about at a conversazione, and during the process the larynx
was stolen !

Facsimile pages of the autograph MS. of "The Imitation of Christ" preserved in the Royal Library at Brussels.

MS. It is described as "a book belonging to the Monastery of the Regular Canons of Mount St. Agnes, Virgin and Martyr, near Zwolle. This, Father John Latomius, a professed member of the Order of Regulars at the throne of our Blessed Lady near Herenthal, and Administrator of the same Order, having visited the Monastery of St. Agnes and rescued from the ruins of the said monastery, to save it from complete destruction, brought to Antwerp, and presented to his old and trusty friend, John Bellère, in the year of our salvation 1577. And John Bellère, further, from his heart presented it to the Fathers of the Society of Jesus, as a thank-offering for his sons, whom in Religion the same Society fosters, on the kalends of June, 1590."

This codex is a small volume of 192 leaves. Two leaves of the original are missing, and were replaced in the sixteenth century by others. It is admitted to be in the handwriting of the author, not by any means a necessary proof of authorship. The claim based on this codex is indeed only an argumentative one. At the beginning there is a table of contents in his handwriting, which supplies the names of thirteen of his own treatises, and it is urged that he would not have included the *Imitation* in such a list were he not the author. The Bishop of Bruges, Mgr. Malou, says that "it is impossible so modest and so pious a writer could have desired to transcribe at the head of his works four very remarkable treatises which were not his own. There are extant several copies of the writer written by his own hand, but there is not one in which his treatises are mixed in the same volume with the works of other divines. By copying the four books at the head of his works he has declared himself to be their author." This seems rather weak, and the plea of "modesty" rather tells the other way, for it would seem modest to place the works of other divines before his own.

It seems, too, that there is also in the Royal Library another MS. in à Kempis' writing, and dated 1425, or sixteen years before the present one, and written at Utrecht. This would be nearer the original, if it be not the original itself. The subject is full of difficulties, and for the general argument little can be founded on it, beyond the fact that Thomas made copies of the work. One argument, however, the little book does furnish, in aid of the theory that the *Imitation* was formed of four separate treatises. For in his table of contents the author so describes it, counting each book as a *libellus*, in company with nine others described in the same way.

Familiar as is the book, it may be suspected that there is scarcely one in a thousand who could tell the real name of the author. Many indeed think that "à Kempis" was his surname, just as the lively author of *The Comic History of England* bore that of "à Beckett." Yet it is merely as though Gerson—the rival claimant—had been styled "John of Paris." The surname signified no more than that the author was "Thomas of Kempen," *i.e., from*, or *of*, Kempen. His real name was Thomas Hammerlain—in learned treatises translated into "Malleolus," or "the Hammer."[1]

We are so familiar with the title, the *Imitation*, that we could hardly be content to accept any other. No one would guess that for a time it bore the odd name of "Church Music," or *De Musica Ecclesiasticâ*, and that a conclave of learned

---

[1] In the British Museum Catalogue you find page after page with works of, and on, this little known mysterious "*Thomas Hammerlain*."

experts, who had met in Paris in 1671, to settle the point of authorship, announced officially that such was the title found in all the most ancient MSS. It declared, also, that the common title had been taken from the initial words of the treatise: *Qui sequitur me non ambulat in tenebris.* This musical name might perplex us as to its meaning or relevancy, but it is not difficult to account for, when we reflect that the author was partial to such fanciful or poetical titles. We have "The Little Garden of Roses," *i.e., Hortulus Rosarum,* "The Garden of Lilies," and such like. "Here begins this little Book," say the doctors, "so consoling for the well-instructed devout. The first chapter is on the Imitation of Christ, and the contempt of the vanities of the world, and formerly they used to give this name to the whole, as though it were a book on the Imitation of Christ. Just as the Gospel of St. Matthew is called the Book of the Generation of Christ, because in the first chapter mention is made of the generations of our Lord." Of this curious Congress a M. de Congé wrote to Dumont, a counsellor of Parliament at Amiens, in August, 1671, that he had assisted at this Council, and that "after all the MSS. that he had seen, he could assert without hazard of veracity, that it was written by Gerson."

Nearly all the MSS. in England—at Oxford, Cambridge, and the Museum—have this title of *De Musica Ecclesiasticâ.* Most of these also support the view that *The Imitation of Christ* refers but to the first section of the work, and there is usually added the more general and fitting description, "Book of Inward Consolation." At Coventry School there is a MS. *De Musica Ecclesiasticâ,* or *Admonitiones ad interna trahentes de internâ consolatione.* The British Museum MSS. are four in number,

D

and have various titles. The Harleian (No. 3,216, anno 1454) begins: *Imi libri opus de perfecta animæ Philosophia.* Most of these English MSS. contain only the three Books. But one has the fourth Book, which is thus described: *De Sacramento Altaris liber unus : qui quartus habebitur de Imitatione.*

This want of homogeneousness seems to have struck the scribes even thus early ; I think, therefore, that we may take it as proved, that the fourth was a detached treatise added on as a sort of supplement.

I have a little pocket edition in Latin, published at Lyons in 1564, which proclaims on the title-page that the work is by "John Gerson, that famous Doctor," but at the foot of the last page it states that, "although this little book is described as being John Gerson's, the author really was Thomas à Kempis, a Regular Canon "—an odd compromise. Here the chapters are not in paragraphs ; with it is printed a much longer work on the contempt of the world, by Dionysius the Carthusian, which thus further emphasizes the second title of the *Imitation.*

A very attractive little edition is the Barbou one, printed and bound in the favourite elegant style of that publisher. All his books are gilt-edged. It is edited by one Velart, who in his Preface points out some gaps and incoherencies which have never been corrected to this day. Thus in chapter vi., book iii., which deals with the "note" of the true lover of God—a continuation from the preceding chapter of the same subject—the topic is suddenly changed at the eighth verse. After declaring that "a generous lover resteth not in the gift, but in *Me* above every gift," the text goes on: "All therefore is not lost if sometimes thou hast not that feeling towards Me and My Saints which thou wouldest have." (The common version, by the way, inserts the words "of devotion" after "feeling" in a rather unmeaning way.) Now these two passages have no connection, and the editor found in the MS. leaves wanting here. Again in chapter xliv., book iii., where the topic is the being dead and indifferent to worldly things, at the fifth paragraph we have, "a temporal loss is bewailed, but spiritual detriment is soon forgotten:" and here something must have dropped out between the passages. So in chapter lvii., book iii.: "Consider the great frailty which thou oftenest experiencest," &c. "Put it out of thy heart as well as thou canst; and if tribulations have touched thee, yet let it not cast thee down," &c. What is to be "put out" is not named; and the text runs, "If it has touched thee." The editor Velart finds that these are corruptions of editors and copyists.

CHAPTER THE FIFTH.

ANALYSIS OF THE FOUR BOOKS—ADMIRABLE RULES FOR SOCIETY—WARNINGS
TO THE STUDIOUS.

N the Trinity College, Dublin, MS. some one has written : "I do hear that this book was made by one Thomas à Kempis : and lett a man looke in any chapter of the said Booke, and he shall find something suteable to his condicion." Indeed the charm of the book, and the reason it has been held in such high esteem in all generations, is surely its *practical* spirit, and the business-like tone of its counsels. It treats the great concern of salvation from a *common-sense* point of view—what indeed has such common sense as saving our soul?—and as though it were something almost professional.

The first Book seems intended as a series of homilies and exhortations addressed to the brethren of the community, whose state is shown to have been a little relaxed, or at least influenced by worldly principles. The remedy is found in the "*following*" of Christ, which can only be done by meditating on His Life. For "the teaching of Christ surpasseth all the teaching of the saints." Here is a hint at that pursuit of theological reading, which he found was too often assumed to be the same thing as practical piety. "But it happeneth that many *from the frequent* hearing of the Gospel, feel little emotion : the reason is because they have not the Spirit of Christ. But he that would fully and with relish understand all the words of Christ, must study to conform his whole life to Him." That is to say, the reading or study of theological matters, with the discussion of refinements, or ardent debate over the comparative merits of the saints, if unsupported by diligent practical piety, is apt to enfeeble practice. The study even of our Saviour's life may leave us cold and indifferent unless that study be supported by "imitation" of that life. This Bishop Butler has shown very clearly in his distinction between active and passive habits. A passive habit, he says, enfeebles the active principle: while *vice versa* the active habit gradually destroys the passive principle.

The whole, then, of this excellent opening chapter seems to exhaust the subject. *Follow Christ*, not in words, or reading, or writing, but in practice, and contemn vanities. Here is struck the note of the whole of the first Book, which is called, "The Book of the Following of Christ." And in the last chapter we find the same note struck again. "Do thou be mindful of the purpose thou hast undertaken *and place before thee the Image of the Crucified.* Well mayest thou be ashamed when looking into the Life of Jesus, that as yet thou hast not studied more to conform thyself to Him." Some theologians, however, have controverted this doctrine of making the imitation of our Lord the "all-in-all" of religious life, contending that it is insisted on too much, thus seeming to make other methods of secondary importance. He shows that the mere relish of the world, or, as he happily puts it, "the love of visible things," is almost destructive. For thus the sense of taste for good is enfeebled—indeed, cannot co-exist with the other. This is in truth one of the great principles of the work, insisted on over and over again, insinuated, impressed in all manner of forms. In his very first chapter he seems to take for his text, "Vanity and all is vanity; but to love God and serve Him *alone.*" Vanity is it, he says, to attend only to the present life, and not to look forward to the things that are to come; to " lift oneself on high ;" to " love what is passing away with all speed." In short, we should " wean our hearts from love. of visible things," for those who follow the pleasure of their senses " sully conscience and lose the grace of God."

These texts are expounded in twenty-five chapters, wherein are inculcated the overcoming or conquest of self; the checking of inordinate affections ; self-restraint ; patience ; the avoidance of the world and its ways ; complete forbearance with others ; and the acceptance of the Cross. It may indeed be said that the grand principles of the book, enforced again and again, are : I. Utter indifference to the attractions of the world. II. Subduing of ourselves. III. Patience with our fellows. IV. The carrying of the Cross. Above all, the sheer impossibility of the co-existence of the love of the world with the love of our Saviour in the same breast. Again and again he enforces the truth, that these are mutually destructive. The one engrosses or devours the other.

The second Book is devoted to the topic of " Interior conversation," and the programme is set out in the first chapter, which again is a summary of the whole. Where, in any book, can we find so compact a summary of religious truth and teaching, as in this short chapter : " The Kingdom of God is within you. *Learn to despise exterior things . . . and thou shalt see the Kingdom of God come within thee*" ? This is a favourite teaching of the author, the "all-in-all" so often insisted on. Here is what is to be done—a difficult thing: and the *way* to do it and the result: "Give then a dwelling-place to Christ, and *refuse entrance to all beside.*" As for men: "They who to-day are with thee, to-morrow may be against thee. . . . Put thy whole trust in God—He will answer for thee." "Why *standest thou looking about thee, since this is not thy place of rest?* All things pass away, and thou, too, along with them. See thou cleave not to them, lest thou be ensnared and perish." Another topic. "If thou knowest not how to meditate on high and heavenly things, rest in the Passion of Christ." "*He whose taste discerneth all things as they are, and not as they are said or accounted to be, is a truly wise man.*" There is a pious cynicism in this, for we feel that nearly all things in the world are "as they are said or accounted to be." "If thou devoutly betake thyself to the precious Wounds of Jesus, thou shalt feel great comfort in tribu- lation: thou wilt not care much for being slighted by man." (We may note the moderation of his "much.") "Christ was willing to suffer, *and darest thou complain of aught?*" "How shall thy patience be crowned *if thou meet with no adversity?*"

The third Book, which is the longest, and perhaps the most important of the three, contains fifty-nine chapters. The opening one thus expounds its subject: "I will hear what the Lord God will speak in me. Happy is the soul that heareth the Lord speaking within her, and receiveth from His mouth the word of comfort. Happy eyes, that are shut to outward things, but intent on things internal. Happy they who penetrate into eternal things," &c. The fourth Book is perhaps the most popular and familiar, dealing with the subject of the Blessed Sacrament in a very practical and even engaging way.

The *Imitation* has one defect; it is so stored with admirable things—all pressed down, compact, running over—which as it were jostle each other, that it is only by accident we come upon what we want. Further, everything is so good that contrast seems wanting, and we are apt to pass by an immense deal that would instantly strike us, did we see it by itself. It is thus that one of Shakespeare's lines affects us when we see it quoted. Nearly every second sentence is worth weighing, and inwardly digesting, if we would gather not only its meaning, but the inner meaning and side-lights, &c. To show what can be done by way of comment, and what has not yet been done, I shall now give a few instances.

One of the best and most practical portions of the book are the rules it supplies for "behaving in society." These directions are simple, almost elementary, needing only the outlay of a little thought. They amount to this: reserve, a guard upon the tongue, with a sense of responsibility in everything said or done. It is indeed a *vade mecum* for all who would "go into the world." First, for the sagacious counsels on "talk." "I would," says our author, "that many a time I had kept silence, and not been in company. *Why are we so fond of speaking and of talking idly together, when yet we seldom return to silence without some wound to conscience?* And we are very fond of speaking and thinking of those things we very much love or wish for, *or that we feel are a contradiction to us.*" How true is this last distinction! Many cannot tolerate that others should even *think* in a way that they do not relish or approve. The suspected existence of this "contradiction" is disagreeable, and an offence. Moreover, "evil custom," and negligence about our spiritual advancement, contribute much to the ungraciousness of our tongue. " Let curiosities alone," he says—an excellent phrase ; and in another place : " *What is this or that to thee?* follow thou Me." "Can't you leave it alone?" said Lord Palmerston once— his remedy for "reforming" many things. "*As often as I have been amongst men,* said one, *I have returned less a man.*" This we too often experience when we talk long. "It is easier to keep silence altogether than not to fall into excess in speaking. It is easier to keep retired at home than to be enough upon one's guard abroad. He, therefore, who aims at inward and spiritual things, must, with Jesus, *turn aside from the crowd.*"

Our author, who seems to have known the world and human nature thoroughly, is specially alive to the mischief of "tale-bearing," or rather of "repeating" things. He dwells even more earnestly on the baleful effect upon the recipient of such stories : "We must not trust every word or impulse, but cautiously and patiently weigh the matter according to God. Alas ! often-times is *evil more readily believed and spoken of another than good;* so weak are we. It is a part of wisdom also, not to believe everything men say, nor straightway to pour into the ears of others what we have heard or believed. Turn thine eyes back upon thyself, and see that thou judge not the doings of others. In judging others a man toileth in vain, *often erreth, and easily sinneth;* but in judging and scrutinizing himself, he always laboureth with profit. We often judge of a thing according *as we have it at heart;* for true judgment is easily lost through private affection. If God were always the only object of our desire, we should not be so easily disturbed at our own opinions being resisted."

It was Talleyrand who said : "*Pour jouir de la vie, il faut glisser sur beaucoup.*" And something of the same thought is found in our author: "It is more profitable *to turn away thine eyes* from such things as displease thee, and leave to every one his own way of thinking, than to give loose to contentious discourses."

And it is curious, too, to see with what originality the theme is varied and presented in different lights: "*If thou canst let men alone, they will let thee alone to do whatever thou hast to do.* Busy not thyself in matters which appertain to others; and entangle not thyself in the affairs of the great. Have always an eye upon thyself in the first place, and admonish thyself preferably to all thy dearest friends. *Sometimes we are moved by passion, and think it zeal.* We blame little things in others, and overlook great things in ourselves."

He thus deals with the discontented busybody: "Many a time he saith what he ought not to say, and leaveth undone that which it were best for him to do. *He considers what others ought to do, and neglecteth that which he is bound to do himself.* Thou knowest well how to excuse and gloss over thine own deeds, but thou wilt not accept the excuses of others. If thou wishest to be borne with, bear also with others. It is no great thing to associate with the good and the gentle; for this is naturally pleasing to all; and every one preferreth peace, and loveth those best that agree with him. But to be able to live peacefully with the hard and the perverse, or with the undisciplined and those that contradict us, is a great grace, and a highly commendable and noble thing."

Admirable is this, and more admirable as we turn it over: "Study, likewise, especially to guard against and *to get the better of such things as oftenest displease thee in others.*" We should note also: "As thine eye observeth others, so again art thou observed by others." I don't know that it has been noticed, that in such sayings there is something of the flavour of La Bruyère and La Rochefoucauld. *"If thou hast any good in thee, believe still better things of others,* that thou mayest preserve humility. It will do thee no harm to put thyself below everybody, but it will hurt thee very much to put thyself before any one." Any one that mixes much in society should study these maxims; if he put them in practice, and most easy they are, he will find himself, almost unconsciously, living a religious life. There is much excellent and practical counsel as to the enduring of prejudice and of ill-natured stories and reports. Great stress is laid on the pain suffered from these depreciating remarks, for which this plain, business-like remedy is offered : "Son, stand firm, and trust in Me; *for what are words but words?* They fly through the air, but hurt not a stone. It is a small matter that thou shouldst sometimes bear with words, who are not able as yet to endure hard blows."

Many of the counsels in the *Imitation* might seem, at first sight, to be "counsels of perfection," and to belong to the higher spiritual life ; but their beauty is they can all be applied to the common current of daily life ; they are so stored with good sense and practical method. For instance, the learned man, the "general reader," the lover of science, the person with the gift of eloquence, will find in one short and precious chapter, the whole philosophy of the thing. To read this occasionally is like taking a tonic.

What sense and wisdom in the warnings given to studious men, even to those engaged in writing in the cause of religion, or, as it was in his day, in the schools. Every reader and student should ponder over these words :

"Never read anything in order that thou mayst appear more learned or more wise.

"When thou shalt have read and shalt know many things, thou must always return to the one beginning.

"*Woe to them that inquire of men after many curious things, and are little curious of the way to serve Me.*

"*The time will come, when Christ, the Master of masters, the Lord of angels, shall appear to hear the lessons of all men.*"

And in another place:

"*The voice of Books is one and the same,* but it teacheth not all men alike, because I within am the Teacher of truth, the Searcher of the heart, the Understander of thoughts, the Mover of actions, distributing in every one as I judge fitting."

Which applies to the *Imitation* itself, for this gives forth its meaning only according to the grace of the reader. Humility, even in championing the Church, is essential. It is astonishing to read in the life of one of its most doughty advocates, that until the close of his life he had all but given up the sacraments. No wonder that John Wesley read a chapter daily; and we learn that the heroic Gordon studied it again and again, and seems to have drawn those high-souled principles of faith and duty which regulated his life.

Special warnings are given against the self-complacency that arises from reading and show of learning. Vain subtleties and discussions, searches into the meaning of the Scriptures, preferences for great saints are discouraged: "Inquire not who may have said a thing, but consider what is said. *God speaketh to us in divers ways, without respect of persons.* Our curiosity is often a hindrance to us in reading the Scriptures."

And how judicious is the distinction taken: "Truly, when

he Day of Judgment cometh, it will not be asked of us *what we
ave read*, but *what we have done ;* not what fine discourses we
ave made, but how religiously we have lived.   Tell me ; where
ow are all those doctors and masters with whom thou wast
ell acquainted while they were yet alive, and in the glory
f their learning ?   Others now hold their preferments, and
  know not whether they ever think of them. ·In their
ifetime they seemed to be something, and now they are not
poken of."

The *Imitation*, like the Scriptures, has, indeed, the power of
ffecting the reader with a sort of inspiration.   According to
he *mood* in which it is read, it reveals " lights " and meanings.
\t one time the passages will appear to be of a conventional
kind ; at another, the same sentence will send forth a flood of
houghts and suggestions. The appreciation must be enlightened
nd quickened by grace or inspiration.   This is beautifully
explained : " Let not Moses, nor any of the Prophets speak to
ne : speak Thou rather, O Lord God, . . . but they, without
Thee, will avail me nothing. They may indeed sound forth
words, but they give not the spirit. Most beautifully do they
peak ; but if Thou be silent, they inflame not the heart. They
publish the mysteries, but Thou unlockest the meaning of the
hings signified. They show the way, but Thou givest strength
o walk in it."

One may admire the pious ingenuity with which the one
heme of the exclusiveness of the worship of God, the impos-
ibility of combining with it the worship of the world, is treated.
This note is fitted to many harmonies. *"All shall perish that
cometh not of God. . . .* Hold fast this short and perfect word :
Forsake all, and thou shalt find all ; relinquish desire, and thou

shalt find rest. . . . If in this life thou seekest rest, how then wilt thou come to the eternal rest. . . . Son, relinquish thyself and thou shalt find Me."

And how plainly and fearlessly is the truth spoken in the following, and with what a stirring eloquence too : " For a long time shall he be little, and lie grovelling beneath, who esteems anything great but only the one, immense, eternal Good. *And whatsoever is not God is nothing, and ought to be accounted as nothing.* There is a great difference between the wisdom of an illuminated and devout man, and the knowledge of a learned and studious cleric. *I know not by what spirit we are led, or what we pretend to, who seem to be called spiritual persons, that we take so much pains and are so full of anxiety for transitory and mean things, and seldom or never think with full recollection of mind on our own inward concernments.*"

CHAPTER THE SIXTH.

NE of the most interesting and curious features of *The Imitation of Christ*, one which has not been investigated hitherto, is the almost personal character of the revelations and communings found in the third Book. This seems to supply a story of mental trouble in the cloister. It may be that there seems to be something rather morbid and exaggerated in these repinings: and the fact is, that no one has more powerfully insisted on the remedies that were at hand. and the opportunities thus offered for obtaining merit. It is not difficult to follow the story. The writer's plain speaking and unsparing reproofs had excited prejudice. He had spoken with relentless severity of the shortcomings of his brethren, who had rather fallen away from their Rule and were given up to vain theological disquisitions, to the neglect of practice. They were eager to go abroad and "gad about," were given over to gossip and tale-bearing, and envious stories, and a neglect of the contemplative life. "The habit and tonsure," he says, "effect but little, but the moral change and the entire mortification of the passions make a true Religious. He *who does not strive to be the least, and subject to all*, cannot long remain in peace." He speaks of "the lukewarm-

ness and negligence of our state : we so soon fall away
from our first state and are' even now tired of life through
slothfulness and tepidity." This was severe. In chapter xviii.
book i. he supplies a contrast between the lives of the older
Religious and that of his brethren, and inveighs against the
constant attempts to escape from the convent and mix with
the world. "Pray for thy sins and negligences. *Leave vain
things to vain people:* look thou to those things which God
hath commanded thee. . . . Stay with Him in thy cell . . . If
thou hadst never left it nor hearkened to any rumours, thou
wouldst have remained longer in happy peace." "Let it seriously
concern thee that thou dost not carry thyself so well and
circumspectly as a servant of God and a devout Religious
ought to do." Such plain speaking could not have been
acceptable.

It is scarcely surprising, therefore, that these rebukes have
been found unwelcome, and that many chapters are full of sad
complaints and sufferings on the score chiefly of trivial tales
and stories repeated against himself. This personal tone might
be considered a defect in this great work : only the treatment
is so large and so very human, that it becomes, as it were,
general. The passage, for instance, "Now he is thought great
who is not a transgressor," has an application for all, if
we but ponder over it: for it seems to present the favourite
current standard of piety. We content ourselves with not abso-
lutely breaking the commandments ; this by contrast with
evil-doers furnishes a sort of claim to merit. The topics from
which he draws comfort show what was the nature of the perse-
cution. In Heaven "no one shall resist thee, no one complain
of thee, *no one obstruct thee,* no one stand in thy way." "Now

therefore bow thyself down humbly under the hands of all. *Heed not who it was that said or commanded this"*—hints, that seem to show us the pious author struggling with himself, and frustrated, mortified, and humiliated, as he strives to effect some reforms.

The average reader who has not carefully studied the work, may naturally consider such a picture as the following to be addressed to the world at large, not to himself in particular: "Sigh and grieve that thou art still so carnal and worldly, so unmortified from thy passions. So much inclined to exterior things; so negligent as to the interior. So prone to laughter and dissipation; so hard to tears and compunction. So inclined to relaxation, and to the pleasures of the flesh; so sluggish to austerity and fervour. So curious to hear news and to see sights; so remiss to embrace humiliation and abjection. So covetous to possess much; so sparing in giving, so close in retaining. So inconsiderate in talking; so little able to hold thy peace. *So disordered in thy manners; so over-eager in thy actions.* So immoderate in food; so deaf to the Word of God. So ready for repose; so slow to labour. So wakeful to hear idle tales; so drowsy at the sacred vigils. So hasty to finish thy devotions; so wandering in attention. So negligent in saying thy Office; so tepid in celebrating; so dry in communicating. So quickly distracted; so seldom fully recollected within thyself. So suddenly moved to anger; so apt to take offence at others. So prone to judge; so severe in reprehending. *So joyful in prosperity; so weak in adversity.* So often proposing many good things; and bringing so little to effect." This, however, was apparently intended as a picture of the community. And here arises the question, Was this in the nature of a private record,

E

as a sort of ease for his feelings: or did he formally lay it before his brethren? In any case, it is a finely outlined sketch, not of the sinner, but of a worldly-minded being. The touchings are masterly.

We can regularly trace the beginning and progress of his trouble. In the first seven chapters of Book iii. the author laments his spiritual difficulties, the failing of his fervour, but he is full of gratitude. "O pleasant and delightful service of God," he exclaims; "O sacred state of religious servitude." But in chapter xii. he begins: "O Lord, *patience* is very necessary for me, . . . for in whatsoever way I may arrange for my peace, my life cannot be without war and sorrow." He is told to "turn away from his own will. He who striveth to withdraw himself from obedience withdraweth himself from grace: and he that seeketh particular privileges loseth such as are in common. . . . Learn then to submit thyself readily to thy Superior," &c.

In chapter xix. he is told, "Do not say, I cannot endure these things from such a man, . . . for he hath done me a great injury, and he upbraideth me with things I never thought of." Still his complaints go on, and he seems to relapse. Then is he bidden to be "not curious, for what is it to him whether each man be such or such, or whether this man speak this or that. . . . Be not solicitous for the shadow of a great name, nor for acquaintance with many, nor for the particular love of individuals." Weaknesses of which he seems to be conscious.

It would almost appear that he was keeping a sort of spiritual diary, setting down day by day the fluctuations of his feelings—now advancing, now going back, now full of hope, now of despondency.   And here may be noted the curiously complex character of the record, for while he formally reproves certain weaknesses in others, it is clear that he himself was equally an offender.   He makes therefore his own particular lapses general, and preaches to himself as well as to others. This mixture gives a reality as well as an originality to the whole.

In a prayer which constitutes the seventeenth chapter, he begs that he may " prudently avoid him that flattereth, and patiently bear with him that contradicteth."   He is told in return not to heed " flying words, to be silent in evil time : not to be eager to please, or fear to displease men."   And so he shall have peace.   All, however, is unavailing, for in the next chapter we find him again sunk in despondency, as " a great tribulation has come upon me."   The stages are indeed almost dramatic, and it would be well worth tracing them day by day.

In the twenty-eighth chapter we find him beginning to pour out his grief.   He is told to " take it not to heart, if some people think ill of thee, and say of thee what thou art not willing to hear . . . whether they put a good or a bad construction on what thou doest."   Thomas then answers that he is " now in tribulation," and that he " is much afflicted with his present suffering."   " Give me patience, O Lord, even at this time. . . . It behoves me to bear it till the storm pass over."

Amid many topics of comfort and wholesome counsels offered, there is this significant one : " I would that . . . thou wert no longer a lover of thyself, but didst simply wait my bidding, *and his whom I have appointed father over thee.*"   Later he is told, " What can any one do against thee by words and injuries "—*i.e.*, calumnies.   " He rather hurts himself than thee

. . . Do not contend with querulous words, . . . so that if at present thou seemest to be overcome, and to suffer a confusion thou hast not deserved, . . . do not lessen thy crown by impatience." He is to "take it not to heart if he sees others honoured and advanced, and himself despised and debased." Still he is constrained to admit, " If I look well into myself, never was any injury done me by any creature."

But in his forty-fifth chapter we have a more precise account of his troubles; and a most curious picture it is. He is in a dreadful state of affliction. He bewails what he suffers from "human fear," and how "the arrows of men's words move him." "Why have I not better provided for my wretched self?" It seems that something was told to him which led him into trouble. "How wisely didst thou forewarn us to take heed of men, in that a man's enemies are those of his own household ; and that we are not to believe if any one should say, Behold here, or behold there. *I have been taught to my cost, and I wish it may serve to make me more cautious, and not increase my folly.*" The incident itself seems, after all, rather trivial. "Be wary," someone had said to him, "keep to thyself what I tell thee. And while I keep silence, and believe the matter to be secret, he himself cannot keep the secret, but betrayeth both himself and me, and goeth his way. From such foolish speech, and such unwary people, defend me, O Lord." His mystery, or silence, on what was now no silence, had brought him disgrace. It must have been a very serious business, for he introduces it with prayers. "Grant me help, O Lord, in my tribulation, for vain is the help of man. How often have I not found faithlessness when I thought I might depend upon it," &c.

One might have thought that this querulousness would have

been treated by one of his own admirable recipes, for, as he often says, it is occasions of this kind that prove a man. That one should confide to the public what he was pledged to keep secret, is indeed evidence of a frivolous character, but such a proceeding usually excites contempt—not certainly indignation. But as I said, our writer, from adhering to his secrecy had probably compromised himself in some way. It is clear that Thomas, gifted as he was, and superior to his brethren, was disinclined to be directed by inferior and dull beings.

Later he again bewails his case. "It is good for me that Thou hast humbled me. . . . It is profitable for me that shame has covered my face, . . . sending disgrace both within and without." In the fifty-second chapter he has arrived at a deep penitence, possibly for his insubordination and groanings. "My mouth can only utter this word, I have sinned. . . . I am worthy of all scorn and contempt." Then he confesses: "I have received from Thy hand the cross. I will bear it. . . . We have begun, we may not go back, nor may we leave off. Take courage, brethren, let us go forward together. . . . For the sake of Jesus we have taken up this cross, for Jesus' sake let us persevere in it."

In the next chapter more light is thrown on the rather trivial character of the disturbance. "Why art thou afflicted at a little matter said against thee? . . . *Thou canst also give good advice*, but when any unexpected trouble cometh at thy own door, then thy counsel and thy courage fail thee." This inconsistency, so manfully confessed, is what gives the extraordinary value to the work. It may be doubted if anywhere else is revealed so candidly this natural weakness of human nature. In all books that profess to teach, the teacher is careful to keep such contradictions out of sight. Our author was clearly a sensitive person, and quick to resent, as we can gather from the advice he puts into the mouth of our Saviour. " Though thou be reluctant to bear it, and feelest indignation, yet repress thyself, and suffer no *inordinate word* to come out of thy mouth."[1]

It may be said that much of Book iii. is thus intended as a picture of Thomas à Kempis' struggles to accommodate himself, to break his soul, to the discipline of his community. At times, and for a few moments, he becomes general, and applies his counsels to Christians at large; but presently the sense of his own battle overpowers him, and he reverts to the personal. This is the key of the whole and makes it really intelligible. All *real* books are thus founded on personal feeling and experience. Thomas found that he could write best, and with the most pointed application, out of his own heart. I have already alluded to an interesting speculation that arises as to what was the original form and purpose of this third Book. Being of so delicate and private a nature, could it have been written as a treatise for general perusal? Could it have been intended for the perusal of his brethren? It might almost seem that it was meant to be in the nature of "Confessions," like that of St. Augustine, and that they were composed for himself, or as a legacy for his companions, to show through what he had passed. But it is clear, I think,

---

[1] There is a passage describing " a certain person," who wished to know that he would persevere, and which is always assumed to apply to the author. I am inclined to doubt this for many reasons, particularly as he has no reticence about his feelings. Further, he uses the ame description in another passage which cannot apply to himself, "a certain person by loving me learned things Divine, and spoke wonders."

that the popular notion of its being merely a portion of the treatise called *The Following of Christ*, is quite an erroneous one; and it almost proves that the Book was compounded of a number of short treatises found in his desk. Further, this may be said. Though few books are more read than the *Imitation*, it is read in a highly superficial fashion, chiefly, I believe, from its being "opened anywhere" and stray passages selected for perusal.

CHAPTER THE SEVENTH.

HE most wonderful thing in this wonderful book is that we can find in it almost everything. It is as though the whole *curriculum* of piety were there. There are principles, maxims, methods, practices, and discipline. If we look for any special point, we are almost certain to find something on the topic. It is like one of the text-books on the sciences, and the whole scheme is set forth as by a professor. The more emotional, too, will find plenty to suit them in the shape of prayers and compunctious visitings. The prayers are "led up to" in an almost dramatic way, introduced at the close of some telling, most effective meditations. But it is a work that requires to be deeply *studied;* mere superficial reading will leave the impression that it is rather a "maze without plan," a heterogeneous mass of pious statements, and "odds and ends." It is best appreciated—on this account perhaps—by the thoughtful and studious. In this view the *Imitation* might be considered the Blackstone of our Catholic constitution. It is the handbook of religious law, right, and obligation. As we ponder over its verities, we feel more and more what a huge and tremendous thing salvation is, how little *sentiment* should enter into it, what a thorough "business" it is. And we must think with doubt and alarm of all those light-hearted, "go-as-you-please" amateurs, who never *think at all* about the matter, and who believe they are doing much if they do not break the Commandments: or, as the author puts it happily: "Now he is thought great who is not a transgressor."

There are devout admirers of the work who, in a difficulty, have recourse to casting the *sortes Kempisenses*, opening a page at random, and seeing what light a third, fourth, or fifth verse will bring. This pious device can hardly fail. In the Life of the interesting and saintly Miss Kerr, we find her affectionate father, who was agitated at the thought of parting with his child when she proposed adopting a religious life, having recourse to this simple method.

Apart from this practical view, passages almost of inspiration are scattered through the book, being full of a noble eloquence and even passion. Let us admire that fine outburst, in chapter xiv. of the third Book, where the author, carried away by a full sense of the Almighty's power and of his own nothingness, breaks into an ennobling and picturesque strain. Yet there is no mere pious rapture here, it is all the sternest realism : "Thou thunderest forth over my head Thy judgments, O Lord, and Thou shakest all my bones with fear and trembling, and my soul is terrified exceedingly. I stand astonished, and consider that the heavens are not pure in Thy sight. If in the angels Thou hast found depravity, and hast not spared them, what will become of me? Stars have fallen from heaven ; and I, dust as I am, how can I presume? They whose works seemed praiseworthy have fallen to the very lowest; and those that did eat the Bread of Angels I have seen delighted with the husks of swine. There is, then, no sanctity, if Thou, O Lord withdraw Thy hand. No wisdom avails, if Thou cease to govern us. No strength is of any help, if Thou cease to preserve us. No chastity is secure without Thy protection. No self-custody profits us, if Thy holy vigilance be not nigh unto us. For, left to ourselves, we sink and perish; but by Thee visited, we are raised up and live. *O weight immense! O sea that cannot be passed over, where I find nothing of myself but only and wholly nothing!* Where, then, is there any lurking-place for glorying? where any confidence conceived of my own virtue? All vainglory is swallowed up in the depth of Thy judgments over me. What is all flesh in Thy sight? Shall the clay glory against Him that formed it? How can he be puffed up with vain talk, whose heart is subjected to God in truth? Neither will he be moved with the tongues of all that praise him, who hath settled his whole hope in God. For even they who speak, behold, they are all nothing, for they shall pass away with the sound of their words: but the truth of the Lord remaineth for ever." What truth and philosophy and good sense—and what poetry too! What a pious euthanasia!

Another enthusiastic passage on suffering and contradic- tion is surely quite as dramatic: "Why standest thou looking about thee here, since this is not the place of thy rest? All things pass away, and thou too along with them. See thou cleave not to them, lest thou be ensnared, and perish. If thou knowest not how to meditate on high and heavenly things, rest in the Passion of Christ, and love to dwell in His sacred wounds. Christ was willing to suffer and to be despised, *and darest thou complain of aught?* Christ had enemies and detractors, and wouldst thou have all to be thy friends and benefactors? How shall thy patience be crowned, if thou meet with no adversity? If thou wilt suffer no contradiction, how *canst thou be a friend of Christ?* Endure with Christ, and for Christ, if thou wouldst reign with Christ." It will be noted how logically this conclusion is introduced.

Yet another fine burst, that really surprises us, is founded on the familiar "I am the Way, the Truth, and the Life," which seems to offer something almost metaphorical from its very familiarity: "Without the Way, there is no going; without the Truth, there is no knowing; without the Life, there is no living. I am the Way which thou must follow; the Truth which thou must believe; the Life which thou must hope for. I am the Way inviolable, the Truth infallible, the Life interminable. If thou abide in My Way, thou shalt know the Truth, and the Truth shall make thee free, and thou shalt attain to life everlasting. If thou wilt enter into Life, keep the Commandments. If thou wilt know the Truth, believe Me; if thou wilt be perfect, sell all. If thou wilt be My disciple, deny thyself. If thou wilt possess a blessed life, despise this present life. If thou wilt be exalted in Heaven, humble thyself in this world. If thou wilt reign with Me, bear the Cross with Me."

In the following is a touch of mysticism, or metaphysical distinction, which is yet intelligible enough and practical: "And what does it concern us about questions of philosophy? He to whom the Eternal Word speaketh is delivered from a multitude of opinions. From the One Word are all things. Without Him no man understandeth or judgeth rightly. He to whom all things are one, who referreth all things to one, and seeth all things in one, may be steadfast in heart, and abide in God at peace.   O Truth! my God! make me one with Thee in everlasting charity."

This simple sense of the great "oneness" or singleness is the note of all that is spiritual; all that is earthy and material is multiple, and crowded with detail. The potency of great writers, such as Shakespeare, is found in this large oneness, which yet abounds in details.   The earth is entirely "things," but appreciation is always as single as an act.

And this leads on to a sentiment often felt, often thought of, but never expressed with such telling force and picturesqueness.   I have quoted it before, but it will bear repeating:

"For a long time shall he be little, and lie grovelling beneath, who esteems anything great but only the one immense Eternal God. *And whatsoever is not God is nothing, and ought to be accounted as nothing.*"

No metaphysician could have put it more accurately. Nothing earthly really *is :* it is as we think it, or suppose it.   At the end it will be like the man who fancied he was saving his precious treasures from a fire, and found in his hands a heap of stones or cinders, which he had perilled his life to carry off.

We shall have by-and-bye one supreme, extra-critical moment, when the logic of this shall flash upon us with the dazzling vividness of a Belshazzar's feast. At the moment of death we shall see its truth, and with amazement at our stupidity at not having seen it before—"*All that is not God is nothing,*" and that this "beautiful earth," as we think it, is nothing but what it is—a great "rag-and-bone" shop!

The origin of all failings he traces to "inconstancy of mind, and little confidence in God."   The man who is careless, and "giveth up in resolution," is tempted in many

ways. And he adds: "Fire trieth iron, and temptation a just
man. We often know not what we can do, but temptation
discovereth what we are." (Here, by the way, occurs one of the
two or three quotations from profane authors found in the book
"*principiis obsta*," which is oddly introduced by "some one has
said.") The precariousness of a "state of feeling" is pointed
out: "Trust not to thy *feeling*: whatever it may be now, it
will be quickly *changed into something else.*" How pointed and
pithy is this. It is as who would say: "*Because* you have this
feeling or humour, pious or otherwise, it is certain to be changed
into something else." And the remedy: "He that is wise,
stands above all these changes, not minding what he feels in
himself, nor on what side the wind of instability bloweth."

Our author dwells particularly on what might seem a trivial
matter, but which has yet a deep importance, viz., the cultiva-
tion of seriousness as a tone of mind, and the avoidance of a
general jocularity on all topics. This sort of unmeaning mirth
in "finding of fun" in most things, is not in any way censurable;
but it tends to produce a frivolous method of viewing serious
things. He reminds us of the tremendous issues that are before
us, and the heavy weight of sin and neglect, and which has to
be borne through life, and which should banish such levities.
So Dr. Johnson, when some clergymen were joking in this fashion,
said to his neighbour: "Sir, this merriment of parsons is highly
offensive." Our author is profuse in his warnings on this head.
"Be not *too free*," he says, "if thou wouldst make any progress,
... and give not thyself up to *foolish mirth.* ... It is wonderful
that any man can ever abandon himself wholly to joy in this
life, when he considereth and weigheth his exile and the many
dangers of his soul." Then he supplies a reason: "Through

levity of heart we feel not the sorrows of the soul, and we often vainly laugh when in good reason we should weep."

And how true is this: "The place avails little if the spirit of fervour be wanting; neither shall that peace stand long, if it be sought from without, and if the state of the heart want the true foundation, that is, *if thou stand not in me : thou mayest change, but shalt not better thyself.*" It would be easy to apply this significant, pointed utterance.

The foundation of all his teaching is this: "In every action and external occupation, be *inwardly free*, master of thyself; that all things be under thee, and not thou under them." Those who enjoy this freedom, "*stand above things present*"—a forcible phrase—"and contemplate the eternal; with the left eye regard things passing, and with the right those of Heaven," and thus seek the end "for which they were ordained by God, and appointed by *that Sovereign Artist*, who has left nothing disordered in His whole creation." "Sovereign Artist" is good; but indeed all his phrases are picturesque and convincing. "Where art thou," he asks, "when thou art not present to thyself?"

He prays that he may "never let the mind slacken from attending to Heaven, and, amid many cares, to pass on as it were without care, not *after the manner of an indolent person*, but by a certain prerogative of a free mind." A happy touch; for this indifference to things may be too often a languor; but there should be an actual exertion. The book abounds in such fine distinctions.

He is fond of using the expressive phrase—this or that "shall not *stand.*" "All self-seekers," that is, even the pious and self-lovers, "are bound in fetters, ... ever unsettled, seeking always their own ease "—*i.e.*, what suits them—" not the things of Jesus Christ, *but oftentimes devising and framing that which shall not stand.*" This is one of his grand principles. We are, as it were, points in the circumference of a circle, whereof God is the centre. Every act should be a line to that centre, and thence come back to the circumference where it touches another point, our neighbour, or oneself, again. In delusive piety the act travels along the circumference to the adjoining point without touching the centre. "All shall perish," he goes on, "that cometh not of God. Hold fast this short and perfect word. Forsake all, and thou shalt find all; relinquish desire, and thou shalt find rest." No wonder he declares that this is not "the work of one day *or children's sport*, but is, as he summarily styles it, "all the perfection of Religious." If it should seem, as naturally it will, too Utopian or impracticable for ordinary persons, we should at least be "*drawn* the more onward towards its lofty heights, *or at least aspire ardently for its attainment.*" It is something to *know* what should be done.

This analysis of the system after which God's blessings are distributed is striking, and perhaps novel. "Though one hath received more, another less, yet all are Thine, and *without Thee not even the least can be had.* He who hath received greater things cannot glory of his own merit, . . . because he is greater and better who attributeth less to himself. But he who hath received fewer ought not to be saddened, . . . but very much praise Thy goodness, because Thou bestoweth Thy gifts so plentifully without respect of persons. All things are from Thee, and therefore Thou art to be praised in all. Thou knowest what is expedient to be given to each ; and why this one has less, and the other more, is not ours to decide, but

Thine, by whom are determined the merits of each." This marvellous book indeed deals with every topic, and in almost every fashion : we find doctrine as well as morals.

Enjoyment of eating and drinking is often thought to be a neutral matter covered by the amiable phrase "a hearty appetite." Yet there is wisdom in this: "Bridle gluttony, and thou wilt the easier bridle every inclination of the flesh."

In another place he says: "Woe to them that inquire of men after many curious things, and are little curious of the way to serve Me. The time will come, when Christ, the Master of masters, the Lord of angels, shall appear *to hear the lessons of all men*, that is, to examine the conscience of every one." The delusion, in short, is that to *do* good things is sufficient ; whereas the whole value depends on the spirit in which they are done.

In one short sentence we often find a suggestion that "gives us pause," and contains a tremendous truth. Witness this: "*He that has My words, and slights them, has that which shall condemn him at the last day.*"

This seems addressed to all pious *amateurs*, to the talkers, and feelers, and sentimentalists, who are no *doers*. But, indeed, it fits us all—"who have My words"—in some shape, and do not translate them into practice. If we were to summarize in a single sentence the essence of true piety, or the *art* of salvation, I think it would amount to what is really the entire thesis of the third Book, varied in innumerable forms: "*Thou canst not both attend to Me, and at the same time delight thyself in transitory things.*" Practice as well as theory, personal introspection and experience, convince us of its truth, veil it as we will. We should at the least *recognize* the truth of it.

Here is a fine recipe for dealing with our neighbours—and

how simple too : " If thou hast any good in thee, do not, as the world has it, claim a just precedence, but "*believe still better things of others.*" The common logic is here put aside—as you are superior, so others are likely to be inferior ; instead of the expected, " As you are first-rate, so you must be better than others," it should run : " Others are likely to be better than thou."

And he adds : " Thou wilt soon be deceived, if thou regard only the external appearance of men. Indeed, if thou seek in others thy comfort and thy profit, thou wilt more often meet with loss. If in all things thou seekest Jesus, truly thou shalt find Jesus ; but if thou seek thyself, thou shalt find thyself also, but to thy own ruin."

His "turns" are often epigrammatic. When we see abundant failings in others, we might turn our eyes away, or not note them, lament them, or think charitably of them. We should " study especially to guard against, and to get the better of such things as," those we chiefly fail in ?—but no—of such as "*oftenest displease thee in others.*" Their fault becomes yours. Connected with which is the following, " As thine eye observeth others, so again thou art also observed by others." Further on he says : " Never think thou hast thyself made any progress *until thou feel thou art inferior to all.*"

F

CHAPTER THE EIGHTH.

TRIALS—SAYING MASS—RECIPE FOR SORROWS.

T would be an interesting thing—perhaps a bizarre thing too—to trace out how the rules of worldly policy, even the general codes of morality, are often opposed to those of piety. Thus we read, "All our peace in this miserable life must be placed rather in humble endurance than in absence of contradiction." Now, the popular idea is that absence of troubles, annoyances, and sorrows, will secure peace; whereas by this holy paradox real peace can only be secured by actual encounter of such things, and letting them pass us "as the idle wind." "Think not, therefore, that thou hast found true peace, if thou feel no burden; nor that then all is well, if thou have no adversary; nor that thou hast attained to perfection, if all things be done according to thy inclination." And again: "He is ready to help them that fight, trusting in His grace; and He, Himself, *provideth us with occasions to fight*, in order that we may overcome." And how suggestive is the following: "With good reason oughtest thou to suffer a little for Christ, since many suffer greater things for the world." It would be difficult to dispose of this plea. And again: "If there had been anything better and more beneficial to man's salvation than suffering, *Christ certainly would have shown it by word and example."* This is novel and striking and well worth pondering over. Again: "Thou oughtest then to call to mind the heavy sufferings of others, and thus thou mayest the easier bear the very little things thou sufferest." Three admirable illustrations or arguments.

"Sweet," says our Shakespeare, "are the uses of adversity," which he so exquisitely likens to the toad, "ugly and venomous," with yet a jewel in its head." This jewel is thus indicated: "Fire, trials, crosses, and temptation prove a just man. We often know not what we can do, but temptation discovereth what we are. *Occasions do not make a man frail, but they show what he is."*

The prevailing cogent logic too of the author is shown in this truly sensible advice. Nothing could be put more pithily; it is here "in a nut-shell:" *"Learn to suffer in little things now*, that then thou mayest be delivered from more grievous sufferings. *Try first here what thou canst bear hereafter."* Also: "From the very same thing whence they conceive delight, thence frequently do they derive the penalty of anguish," which Shakespeare may have seen when he wrote: "The gods, of our pleasant vices make whips to scourge us."

There are various ways and fashions of "saying" the Holy Mass. Some linger, slowly and laboriously, over its rites and ceremonies; others hurry through it "post haste." How sagaciously the author suggests the true *juste milieu:* "Be neither too slow nor too quick in celebrating; but observe"—not personal humour or fancy, but—"*the good common medium of those with whom thou livest."* That is, if they are busy working-folks, be brisk and energetic; if they are not over-zealous and come but rarely, make the sacrifice inviting, by a certain promptness and animation, so that they shall not be repelled. "Thou oughtest not to *beget* tedium or weariness in others, but *keep the common way.*"   In short, here is the golden rule—"Rather accommodate thyself to *the utility of others* than follow thine own devotion and affection."   This precept almost gives us a higher opinion of the good sense and wisdom of the author than anything else.

He does not content himself—as pious writers sometimes do —with dwelling on weaknesses and failings, but always goes on to point out a remedy, a particular course.   "Oh, how great is human frailty which is ever prone to vice!   To-day thou confessest thy sins, and to-morrow thou again committest what thou didst confess; now thou preparest to be on thy guard, and an hour after thou art acting as if thou hadst made no resolu- tion."   To find a remedy he goes to the very root of the matter —not to fresh resolutions, or new efforts and exertions of strength : but to make admission that we have no strength and no resolution!   For we must "*humble* ourselves, and never think anything great of ourselves."   Having made this discovery, and being convinced of its truth, we may set to work afresh.

Excellent and admirable as no doubt are the regular "good- doers," committee folk, cheque drawers, and the like, yet such will find little harm in giving a few moments' meditation to the following, and in applying the text indicated.   The popular notion is that such things are convincing evidences of piety. But hear our Thomas on the point.   "Do they not," he asks, "prove themselves to be rather lovers of themselves, than of Christ, who are always thinking of their own advantage and gain?"   This he explains : "Many secretly seek themselves in what they do, and are not aware of it.   They seem also to continue in good peace so long as things are done according to their will and judgment; but if aught happens otherwise than they desire, they are soon disturbed and become sad." The slight ironical flavour here will be noted, as well as the almost sarcastic description of the " mood" of the person " disturbed and become sad," that is, " put out " as it is called, or even " ill-humoured."

There have been many meditations on death. Our author, instead of the more conventional topics, touches on what is most likely to affect the careless and unthinking. " If thou hadst a good conscience, thou wouldst not fear death. . . . If thou art not prepared to-day, how wilt thou be to-morrow? . . . Of what use is it to live long when we advance so little. . . . *Would that even for one day we had behaved ourselves well in this world!* . . . When thou art sick, I know not what thou wilt be able to do. *Few are improved by sickness.*" " If thou art not solicitous for thyself now, who will be solicitous for thee hereafter? The time will come when thou wilt fain implore one day or even one hour for amendment, and *I know not if thou wilt obtain it.*"

" Ah, fool! why thinkest thou to live long when thou art not sure of one day?" The most practical of these counsels is, should we see another die, to make profit of the spectacle. It is really the next thing to our own death, a " rehearsal" as it were. It might be our own, it must be and will be our own. Yet the fashion is to shun such spectacles, to cover up the subject: only to make the shock and surprise greater.

" Trust not in thy friends and neighbours (*i.e.*, for prayers for the dead), for men will forget thee sooner than thou thinkest, . . . if thou art not solicitous for thyself."

He has one fine, eloquent passage on this subject of death,

which I am tempted to give here in one of the old English versions. The grand "ring" of the diction is worthy of the original:

"Tell me now, where are the lords and masters that thou knewest sometime, while they lived and flourished in the schools. Now other men have their prebends, and I wot not whether they once think upon them. In their lives somewhat they appeared: and now of them speaketh almost no man. O Lord, how soon passeth the glory of this world! Would God that their life had been according to their cunning, for then had they well studied and well read. How many be there that perisheth in this world by vain cunning, that little recketh of the service of God! And for they chose rather to be great than meek, they vanished away in their own thoughts."

He notices how seldom we weigh our neighbour in the same balance as ourselves. And then comes this striking argument: "*If all were perfect, what then should we have to bear from others for the love of God?*

"Whatsoever thou reposest in men, out of Jesus, thou wilt find to be well-nigh lost. Trust not, nor lean upon a reed full of wind. . . . He that clingeth to the creature shall fall with the creature. . . . Sooner or later, thou must be separated from all, whether thou wilt or no."

Volumes have been written on the subject of " Bearing our Cross," but it may be doubted if anything more practical, picturesquely eloquent, or more convincing has been furnished than what is found in the twelfth chapter of Book iii. This of course is the direct fruit of the imitation of our Lord.

"To many this seemeth a hard saying: 'Deny thyself, take up thy cross and follow Jesus.' But it will be much harder to hear that last word: 'Depart from Me, ye cursed, into ever-lasting fire.' Why, then, art thou afraid to take up thy cross, which leadeth to the Kingdom? If thou fling away one cross, without doubt thou wilt find another, and perhaps a heavier. Dost thou think to escape that which no mortal ever could avoid? For even our Lord Jesus Christ Himself was not for one hour of His Life without the anguish of His Passion. Take up, therefore, thy cross, and follow Jesus and thou shalt go into life everlasting. Go where thou wilt, seek what thou wilt, thou shalt not find a higher way above, nor a safer way below, than the way of the Holy Cross. Dispose and order all things according as thou wilt, and as seemeth best to thee; and thou wilt still find something to suffer, either willingly or unwillingly; and so thou shalt always find the Cross. Prepare thyself to suffer many adversities and divers evils in this miserable life; for so it will be with thee, wherever thou art, and so indeed wilt thou find it, wheresoever thou hide thyself. It must be so, and there is no remedy against tribulation and sorrow, but to bear them patiently. Drink of the chalice of thy Lord lovingly, if thou desirest to be His friend, and to have part with Him. No man is fit to comprehend heavenly things who hath not resigned himself to suffer adversities for Christ."

" Neither canst thou be delivered or eased by any remedy or comfort; for as long as it shall please God, thou must bear it. The Cross, therefore, is always ready, and everywhere awaiteth thee. Turn thyself upward, or turn thyself downward; turn thyself inward, or turn thyself outward; everywhere thou shalt find the Cross. If thou carry the Cross willingly, *it will carry thee*, and bring thee to thy desired end, namely, to that place where there will be an end of suffering, though here there will be no end. If thou carry it unwillingly, thou makest it a burden to thee, and loadest thyself the more, and nevertheless thou must bear it."

I have quoted his plain speaking: "Whatsoever thou reposeth in men out of Jesus, *thou wilt find to be well-nigh lost.*" Then in another form: "The soul that loveth God, despiseth all things *that are less than God.*" And again: "In proportion as a man *draws things* to himself, just so much is he hindered and distracted." How different are these expressions, and this "way of putting things," to the conventional forms?

He has some short terse maxims that can be borne in the memory, and thus made profitable; such as these three: "Ever keep in mind thine end, and that time lost returneth no more. Without care and diligence, thou shalt never acquire virtues. If once thou beginnest to be lukewarm, *thou beginnest to be in a bad state.*"

This last warning is significant: lukewarmness leads to relaxation, relaxation to abandonment; while after abandonment rarely is there a return to the former state.

How good and sound is what follows: "No man can safely appear in public, *but he who loves seclusion.* No man can safely speak, *but he who loves silence.* No man can safely be a superior, but he who hath learned how to obey well." The world's principle is a totally opposite one, . . . at all events, it puts aside the "safely," which is the main point of the whole. The man who talks, hates silence; the social shun solitude; and those who rule, disdain service.

That pride which is so commonly felt in talents, gifts, worldly possessions, &c., as though these were of one's own making, is treated in this sagacious common sense way: "Trust not in thine own knowledge, nor in the cunning of any man living, but rather in the grace of God, who helpeth the humble and *humbleth them that presume upon themselves."* It may be remarked how few accept the notion that such "humbling" really takes place: there is a sort of worldly blindness which assumes that such casualties are to be accounted for by anything rather than by Divine interference. Yet if we look round we shall every day see instances of this sort of chastisement overtaking the arrogant. "Boast not thyself," he goes on, "of thy stature or beauty of body, which with a little sickness is spoiled and disfigured. Be not proud of thy abilities, or thy talents, lest thou offend God to whom appertaineth whatever good thou mayest naturally have. Esteem not thyself better than others, lest perhaps thou be accounted worse in the sight of God who knoweth what is in man. Be not proud of thy own good works: *for the judgments of God are others than those of men."*

The true philsophy of pious action and pious life finds expression in the following: "He doth much who loveth much. He doth much who doth well what he does (*i.e.*, be it ever so little). He doth well who regardeth rather the common good than his own will." Because "oftentimes that seemeth to be charity (or piety), which is rather of the flesh, natural inclination, self-will, hope of reward, study of interest, will seldom be absent," whereas the truly devout "seeks himself in nothing, but only desires God to be glorified in all things." Yet there are thousands of "good persons," who never give this distinction a thought. As our author makes our Saviour say, "*I am the prover of all the devout."*

But too often, indeed, with a number of persons the

outward and visible sign of piety is placed in attendance at religious offices. A person who finds a relish in such things is apt to beguile himself, or oftener herself, into the conviction of his or her goodness. For, says our author: "If we place our religious progress in outward observances only, *our devotion will soon come to an end.*" This is plain speaking: and yet the result is only too certain. The cynic might often be entertained with the spectacle of eager passionate devotees who cannot have too much of rites and "observances," and will forecast the too certain issue. The doer is content with himself: then comes a relaxing based on this self-content and final abandonment. And he has little strokes and touches which show a profound knowledge of the grand religious science: as when he speaks of that disgust or despondency when some failure or fall takes place—when it is fancied that "it is no use" going on, in such a situation. "All is not lost" he tells us—(which describes exactly the feeling). "Man thou art and not God—thou art flesh, not an angel. How canst thou continue ever in the same state of virtue when this was wanting to the angels and to the first man. I am He who raiseth up them that mourn: and them that know their own infirmity, *I promote* to My *own divinity.*" Could anything be more practical or pointed? Those who seize and welcome such opportunities are "promoted to our Lord's divinity"—one of his happy phrases. This is a good illustration of the solid things that are to be found in the Book, but which have to be sought for. In another place he tells us, "Some only carry their devotions in their books, some in pictures, and some in outward signs and figures. Some have Me in their mouths, while there is little of Me in their hearts." We have a further test of genuine devotion. "He that knoweth how to walk interiorly and to make little account of things external, *doth not look for places nor wait for seasons* to perform exercises of devotion."

Nor should we feel ourselves too secure. "For all that is high is not holy: nor is every pleasant thing good: nor every desire pure: nor is every thing that is dear to us pleasing to God." Such are fine thoughts, devotional feelings, general philanthropy, or the wish to do grand spiritual things, which the superficially pious so often mistake for the genuine article. On the contrary, our author seems to hold that coldness, absence of feeling, and a sense of what is disagreeable or even painful, are better "notes" of its presence. "It is much, and very much," he tells us, "to be able to forego all comfort, both human and Divine— to be willing to bear this interior banishment for God's honour."

The proper religious view of things brings a sort of Divine light—or, as he so often says, it is the seeing things "as they are, not as they appear to be." "If only thy heart were right, then every created thing would be to thee a mirror of life and a Book of holy teaching. There is no creature so vile as not to manifest the goodness of God." The failure not to see this is thus explained: "If thou wert inwardly good and pure, then wouldst thou discern all things without impediment and comprehend them aright. A pure heart penetrates Heaven and Hell. According as every one is interiorly, so doth he judge exteriorly." How forcible is all this: what shrewd common sense is here: how plain and clear the explanation.

As I noted at the beginning, Shakespeare must have read his *Imitation*, and seems to have reproduced this very passage in the oft-quoted verses, sermons in stones, books in running brooks, and good in everything; "There is no creature so vile," &c., surely suggested the beautiful lines in the *Merchant of Venice.*

"The senses of men are often deceived in giving judgments; and *the lovers of this world are deceived in loving only visible things.* How is a man a whit the better for being reputed greater by man? The deceitful deceiveth the deceitful, the vain deceiveth the vain, the blind the blind, the weak the weak, as often as he extolleth him; and, in truth, doth rather confound him, whilst he vainly praiseth him. For *how much soever each one is in Thy eyes, so much is he and no more,* saith the humble St. Francis."

It is only by pausing to weigh carefully and meditate over his words, that we see how much teaching may be contained within some apparently conventional phrase. Thus we are often enjoined to "leave all to God," to "place ourselves in His hands," &c. But our author's phrase has a fine, powerful significance. "*For at too great hazard doth he stand,* who casteth not his whole care on Thee:" where the words chosen seem to convey something of alarm and peril. Speaking of our Saviour's Life and example, he says forcibly enough. "If Thou hadst not gone before and instructed us, *who would have cared to follow?*"

"Look upon the lively examples of the Holy Fathers, in whom shone real perfection and religion, and thou wilt see how little it is, yea almost nothing, that we do." That is, look at all the labours of the truly holy, their unending toil, their self-denials, fastings, and perpetual *service* of God; and the whole thought but little of, as a claim for salvation. Then turn to the easy-going meagre efforts of ourselves, or of the average Christian. Yet we look for the same reward!

Another of his pithy truths, "Thou art valiant enough, so long as no adversity comes in thy way," refers to the commonest of delusions. Everything is going "beautifully," rites, sacraments, spiritual unction, prayers, novenas, retreats, &c. We are valiant enough, when suddenly comes a contradiction, and the whole "jerry built" structure collapses in a cloud of dust and rubbish. The foolish turn away in disgust and leave the ruin there; the more sensible, much humiliated and full of shame, will rebuild at once in different fashion. "We are all frail;" as who should say, "we are all miserable sinners."[1] There is here a faint assumption of superiority, even in the best. But we are hardly prepared when our author adds bluntly: "But none is more frail than thyself."

Every one's experience will tell him that failure, the being crossed and mortified, certainly tends to seriousness, to earnestness, and to inward thought. As à Kempis says: "They often make a man enter into himself that he may know that he is in exile." This brings us nearer to God, "for then we the more *earnestly seek God to be witness of what passes within us.*" That is, it gives a sudden *reality* to our conception of the Almighty, what before was somewhat of an abstract idea.

Then we have an admirable recipe for the bearing of crosses, annoyances, and trials, and one most constant and efficacious, in the words: "Thou oughtest, then, to call to mind the heavier sufferings of others, that thou mayest the easier bear the very little things thou sufferest. The better thou disposest thyself for suffering, the more wisely dost thou act, and the more dost thou merit; and thou wilt bear it more easily if both in mind

---

[1] The late Master of Trinity had much of this penetrating, sarcastic spirit, as when he said: "We are none of us infallible, *not even the youngest of us.*"

and body and by habit thou art diligently prepared for it." That is a comparison with the more terrible trials of our friends, and which will almost invariably show how slight our own are. How sensible, too, the advice to prepare and *practise* ourselves for sufferings, a practice that will furnish stays and props for the strain when it comes. The wise man will *rehearse* his own behaviour in presence of such things, and of his death even.

His reversal of popular judgments is often pointed and curious, and furnish surprises: as, "If thou shouldst see another openly do wrong or commit some grievous sins, thou needst not think thyself better, for thou knowest not how long thou mayest be able to persevere in well doing."

CHAPTER THE NINTH.

VAINGLORY—SERVING GOD "DISINTERESTEDLY"—SOME MODEL PRAYERS—PIOUS
ROUTINE—INTELLECTUAL SHIPWRECKS, &c.

TO his brief and pointed question: "What is the truth by which all vainglory is put to flight?" he answers: "We have nothing to pride ourselves on; for everything is given, or can be taken away, by God." "Principally refer all things to Me, for it is I that have given thee all. . . . Therefore all must be returned to Me as to their origin. . . . Therefore thou must not ascribe any good to thyself, *nor attribute virtue to any man*, but give all to God, without whom man has nothing. I have given all, *I will also have all again.*" So true is this in the history of the world, it might be said that this "taking away" is far more common than giving. That attributing virtue to any man is a moral reflection, for even if we rate ourselves properly we are apt to admire the gifts of others, as though they were their own. Here is a striking thought on the same subject: "Behold all things are Thine which I have and with which I serve Thee, and yet contrariwise Thou rather servest me than I Thee." And again: "If thou considerest the dignity of the Giver, no gifts will seem too little or too mean for thee. For that is not little which is given by the Most High God. Yea, though He give punishment and stripes; for whatsoever He suffereth to befall us, He always does it for our salvation."

" *Where shall we find,*" he asks, " *a man who is willing to serve God disinterestedly ?* If a man gives his whole substance, still it is nothing. And if he do great penance, it is but little. And if he attain to all knowledge, he is far off still. And if *he have great virtue and very fervent devotion*, there is still much wanting to him. What is that? That having left all things else, *he leave also himself,* and when he shall have done all things he knows he ought to do, let him think he has done nothing." We commonly hear of lifting ourselves from the attractions of earthly things, and there seen the contradiction of persons seemingly engrossed in pious things, yet also strangely worldly when the occasion arises. Our author's analysis of this state is acute. He explains it: " He that is weak in spirit . . . and inclined to things of sense, cannot without difficulty separate himself wholly from earthly desires." Though he may follow rule and order, there are notes which betray his old leaning. " He is sad when he does withdraw himself," *i.e.*, sacrifice his whim, " and he is easily moved to anger if any one thwart him." If he check himself, that is, he is discontented, but if another checks him he is angered. Further, if he yield to his whim, he begins to feel compunction, so that in all the cases there is trouble and disturbance. The only true peace is in restraint and indifference to things of the senses. It is in interior pictures of this kind that our author excels.

Many rather pusillanimously avoid temptations. He explains that dangerous occasions are not to be sought, but if they present themselves are to be confronted manfully and with certain profit. For he says: "Many seek to fly temptations and fall the more grievously into them. *By flight alone we cannot overcome.* He who only shunneth sins outwardly and doth not pluck out their root will profit little ; nay, temptations will the sooner return." As when a horse " shies," the judicious rider will not hurry him from the spot, but will lead him gently back and quietly make him confront the danger until he grow familiar with it.

In another place he says, that " some are preserved from great temptations and are often overcome in daily little ones, that thus they may never presume upon themselves in great trials, when they are weak in such trifling occurrences." We might almost fancy, indeed, that a person who is only saved from sin by the occasion not presenting itself, is well-nigh as accountable as an actual delinquent.

With many persons there is a good deal of *routine* in their pious exercises. But it will not do to be merely *passive*. For, " as our *purpose* is, so will our progress be, and he hath need of much diligence who wishes to advance much." Each day's work and acts should therefore be a new effort. Every " Our Father " even should be recited with all the freshness of a first effort. Yet it is to be feared there is no prayer which is said so mechanically or inattentively. He goes on : " And if he who strongly purposeth doth yet oftentimes fail, what will he do *that seldom and but weakly resolveth ?* The falling off from any good resolution happeneth many ways, and a trifling omission in our exercises *hardly passeth over without some loss.* The resolutions of the just depend rather on the grace of God than on their own wisdom."

Of the prayers into which the author of the *Imitation* occasionally breaks, not too much can be said in praise, for their vigour and robustness and direct " coming to the point." It is as in the common life, when some blunt and sincere person

G

states his case and what he wants in the plainest terms. We
may contrast this strain with the conventional strain of
modern prayers, and their exaggerated forms, " Let me die a
thousand deaths rather than," &c., which is somewhat insincere.
Take this as a specimen, a prayer for earnestness and the
feeling of "reality" in religious things: " O Light Eternal!
transcending all created lights, dart forth that light from above
which may penetrate all the secret recesses of my heart.
Cleanse, cheer, enlighten, and enliven my spirit with its powers,
that with joyful ecstasy I may cleave to Thee. So long as this
is not granted, my joy will not be full. As yet, alas, the old
man is living in me; he is not wholly crucified, he is not
perfectly dead. He still lusteth strongly against the spirit, he
wageth war within me, neither suffereth he the kingdom of the
soul to be quiet. But Thou, who rulest over the power of
the sea, and assuagest the motion of its waves, arise and help
me. Show forth, I beseech Thee, Thy wonderful works, and
let Thy right hand be glorified. For there is no hope nor
refuge for me but in Thee, O Lord my God. Behold a temporal
cross is bewailed; for a small gain men *labour and run*, but
spiritual detriment is soon forgotten and hardly ever returns to
mind, . . . for the whole man *sinketh down into outward* things,
and unless he quickly recovereth himself, he willingly continues
immersed in external things."

The very last sentence in the *Imitation* is full of significance
and is singularly applicable at the present moment: "If the
works of God were such that they could be easily comprehended by human reason, they could be called neither wonderful,
nor unspeakable." That is to say, all attempts at explaining
the great mysteries of faith, so as to be intelligible: for clear

explanation takes them out of the supernatural order, and brings them down to the measure of earth. . . . For their full understanding we must wait till we enter another sphere. Nowadays, however, we seem to treat such mysteries as "open questions"—to be discussed, supported, or refuted—in *Contemporary Reviews*, *Nineteenth Centurys*, and such organs, as though they were questions of politics, or political economy. Such was that repulsive theory started by a certain professor, not long since, of "Happiness in Hell," which was seriously encountered by the orthodox and shown to be untenable. It was in truth beyond and above discussion—at least by those holding the same faith, and certainly savoured of heterodoxy. The good honest old Dr. Johnson would not so much as stay in the room with a notorious infidel like Dr. Priestley: he even maintained that in dealing with such persons, you were not bound to treat them with the ordinary courtesies of discussion. They were like persons who wanted to rifle you of your property.

The devoting oneself to such inquiries is indeed a fashion of the day: and the orthodox are busy championing their doctrines, replying and retorting on the enemies of the faith. It has been noted that there is a serious danger in this: that such speculative matters are apt to draw away from practical efforts and real religious exertion. A Kempis expounds this in the most sagacious way. "Many have lost devotion," he says, "while they would pry into lofty matters. . . . God is able to effect more than man is able to understand. Blessed is the simplicity which leaves *the difficult path of questionings* and goeth on to the plain and sure path of God's commandments." Then he asks pertinently: "If thou dost neither understand or comprehend these things which are beneath thee, how mayest thou comprehend such as are above thee. . . . God walketh with the simple, revealeth Himself to the humble. He discloses His meaning to the pure and hideth His grace from the curious and proud." Controversy tends to pride, " puffing up," and to the neglect of practical life. The *quid nunc* politician is found to neglect his business, while he is settling the affairs of the nation.

A notable instance of such shipwreck, exactly illustrating the author's words, is that of the Abbé de La Mennais, who translated the *Imitation* anew in 1830, and added "reflections" of his own, in substitution of the still popular comments of Gonnelieu. His remarks on the book are rather original, and some are specially characteristic when considered in connection with his unfortunate catastrophe. " It has been remarked," he says, "that the *Imitation* is a book for the perfect; but it is all the same useful for beginners. Nowhere can we find a deeper knowledge of man, his contradictions, his weaknesses, and the secret turnings of his heart."

He sagaciously adds this caution : " We must not expect it to produce these lively and sudden impressions, and a salutary change—the *Imitation* requires the heart to be prepared." We may be affected in this way—admire the power of thought and language, and yet no change may follow. He then adds a most significant warning—considering his own unhappy case—" Nothing will help to salvation, that is not founded on *humility*. If you are not humble, or at least do not desire to be so, the word of God will fall on your heart like water on sand. To believe in yourself, and to love yourself only, is pride. Humble yourself then, and faith and love will be given us : humble yourself and salvation shall reward us for the victory gained over pride."

Remarkable words indeed ! The world knows, it was this pride that was to make shipwreck of the unhappy man. The notes at the end of each chapter are conventional enough, and certainly not superior to those of Gonnelieu.

To show its magic influence, he quotes La Harpe's description of its effect on him. He was in prison, expecting death, and without any resources. He had read the Psalms and the Gospels, and was, as he said, restored to the faith; but he trembled as he looked back on his forty years of sin and neglect, and dreaded the judgments of God. He found nothing to comfort or reassure him. Suddenly he opened the *Imitation*, and his eyes fell on this passage : " Here am I, My son, I come to you because you have called Me." The prisoner fell on his face on the ground, and shed torrents of tears, uttering broken cries and sobs. Never did he feel his heart touched so poignantly, or did he experience such exquisite emotions— the words seem to ring for ever in his ears. The passage is a long one and the description very minute ; but it is obvious that there was nothing very striking in the passage, the sense of which he must have encountered in many forcible turns in his Scripture readings. It is indeed virtually a quotation, and a rather trite one.

What sagacity and insight in the following : " For all that is high is not holy, nor is every pleasant thing good, nor every desire pure, nor is everything that is dear to us pleasing to God." Superficial piety is here accurately described. It thinks all fine high emotions, holiness ; it takes pleasing feelings of devotion to be the same thing as "goodness ;" it supposes that its grand schemes and purposes are " pure ; " that is an anticipation of the will of God, whereas they come from one's own will ; and greatest mistake of all, that what we " like " to do, must be what God likes.

In this connection he says in another place: " Let nothing then seem too much to thee of all thou doest." " *Because of thyself, thou always tendest to nothing,*" that is, the natural direction is downwards. On the slightest relaxation we tend to nothing. " Speedily dost thou fail, speedily art thou *over-powered*, speedily *disturbed*, speedily *dissolved.*" Who has not felt that almost magical, and most mortifying catastrophe. As you advance in smiling complacency, in an instant the fabric has toppled over and lies in ruins ; all resolutions, prayers, exercises, pieties, are as though they had never been. It is a general wreck. Nothing however is so wholesome as such a disaster. These ill ballasted pietists on such a shock will often "throw up the game." The genuine devotee differs in this, that if he fall through such frailty, he "resumes greater courage than before," confiding in Heavenly aid. " All therefore is not lost, if thou hast not sometimes the feeling towards me that thou wouldst have."

Pious persons of a certain sort will conceive many a religious scheme, or good work. But, says our author, " The resolutions of the just depend rather on the grace of God, than on their own wisdom, and in Him they put their trust whatever they take in hand." There is the test and "note" of genuine piety. The works are done not for ourselves, or because we fancy them, but for God. To the same class applies another of his sayings: "take care not to be slothful in what is common, and too ready to do what is singular." How much do we see "fads" in short, taken up and pursued vehemently, because novel and interesting; ordinary things neglected, because uninteresting and humdrum. It will be seen from these instances how thoroughly he had searched the corners and crannies of the human heart. Thus according to his picturesque, forcible expression, which he allots to our Saviour: "I am *the mighty Prover of the devout*." That is, the truly pious are ready to have their works tested, tried by sorrow and suffering and a hundred ways.

CHAPTER THE TENTH.

THE JUDGMENT—"ROBUSTNESS" OF THE PRAYERS—GRATITUDE FOR THE
LEAST—"THE GOOD PEACEABLE MAN," &C.

UR author sets before us with almost pictorial
effect some great religious scenes, to which he
imparts an abundance of touches, often poetical,
but more often telling and forcible. Witness
his plain straightforward account of the Judgment. "In all
things look to the end, and how thou wilt stand before the
strict Judge, from whom there is nothing hid; who takes no
bribes and *receives no excuses.* O most miserable and foolish
sinner, what wilt thou answer unto God, who knoweth all thy
evil deeds—*thou who art sometimes afraid of the countenance of
an angry man.* Better is it to purge away our sins, and cut off
our vices now, than to keep them for purgation hereafter." This
being "sometimes afraid of an angry man" is a home thrust,
and brings the final scene before us in most graphic style.

The subject of the Judgment Day has been treated in many
forms. Yet there is one idea suggested by our author in this
connection that has always struck us as something original and
telling. "Why dost thou not provide," he asks, "against the
Day of Judgment, *when no man can be excused or defended by
another?*" Here below we have always the idea of *help* to be
secured by money or affection; of a crowd round us, when

some one will come to our aid, &c. But here we have the notion of the grand solitude of that awful day, and our complete helplessness, when "no man can be excused or defended by another." It calls up the scene in a chilling way.

In the few following sentences, we find a regular scheme indicated ; he often thus sketches, as it were, in brief sentences some of the momentous elements of a Religious life. He begins : "Never desire to be singly praised or beloved ;" *i.e.,* to have a preference or be put above others. The reason is unexpected, "for this belongeth to God alone, who hath none like unto Himself." No one of us therefore can claim to be superior to his fellows. "Neither desire that any one's heart should be much taken up with thee, nor do thou be much taken up with the love of any one, but let Jesus be in thee and in every good man. Thou must be naked and bear a pure heart towards God, if thou wilt be free to experience how sweet the Lord is." This is never to be attained unless by the aid of grace, "when thou hast dismissed and cast out all others."

We are familiar with the conventional prayers found in good books, their rather meaningless repetitions and common forms. About the *Imitation* prayers there is a fine robustness, a practical coming to the point and directness that is extraordinary. Consider, for instance, all that is compressed and packed into the following : "Enlighten me, O good Jesus, with the brightness of internal light. Restrain my many wandering thoughts. Fight strongly for me and overcome the wild beasts . . . that peace may be made in Thy power and the abundance of Thy praise may resound in Thy holy court— that is, in a clean conscience. . . . Lift up my mind oppressed with the load of sin and raise my whole desire towards heavenly

G *

things ; that having tasted the sweetness of supernal happiness, I may have no pleasure in thinking of the things of earth. . . . Join me to Thyself with an inseparable bond of love ; for Thou alone art sufficient for souls that love Thee, and without Thee all other things are frivolous."

He insists on the ordinary *decent* expression of gratitude to Almighty God for the shower of daily blessings which every individual enjoys.   This should never be interrupted, for, if we think of it, we shall see that it is a fresh renewal of favours. With Almighty God, not to take away is to give.   Everything tends to depart from us or to decay—health, fortune, happiness, good spirits, the sense of appreciation ; on which hear our author.   "Be grateful, then, for the least, and thou shalt be worthy to receive greater things. *Let the least be to thee as something very great, and the most contemptible as a special favour.*   If thou considerest the dignity of the **giver, no** gift will seem little or too mean for thee.   For that. is not little which is given by the most high God."   How beautiful is this, and, above all, what a genuine spirit of religiousness is here !

No other writer, as I have shown, seems so practical, or offers counsels so suitable to all classes.   If we cannot go by the perfect way, we must strive at something lower.   The author is fond of setting forth the great virtue of " disposition," where we are too feeble for acts.   " *Dispose thyself* to patience rather than to consolations."   And again : " The better thou disposest thyself for suffering the more wisely dost thou act, and thou wilt bear it more easily if both in mind and by habit thou art diligently prepared for it."   "*Dispose thyself,*" that is, expect trouble as your lot.   Rehearse it, try your strength, and fancy how you will bear.   Wonder gratefully that you have escaped so far. In other words, hold that our present state is but precarious, and can be changed in an instant—what we see every day about us—into something disastrous. The easy-goers take the opposite course, assuming that their present comfort will continue, and that if change come, it will be by some unlucky accident.

Here is an analysis of the mental processes that attend eager desires and longings. "Whenever a man desires anything inordinately," there follows—what? Not hope, or enjoyment, or anticipation, but "straightway he is disquieted within himself." There may be those who would wish to check or crush such longings, but these are often "soon tempted to overcome in little and paltry things." This is because they are "weak in spirit and inclined to *things of sense.*" In this state, when such a one does restrain his desires, the result is that "he is often sad ; and besides, *he is easily moved to anger if any one thwarts him.*" On the other hand, if he yield, "he is burdened with remorse of conscience for having gone after his passion, which helpeth him not at all to the peace he looked for." This is a quaint but true picture of the half-hearted pious person, "who would run with the hare and hunt with the hounds." And the conclusion is that there is no peace in the heart of the carnal man, "nor in the man *who is devoted to outward things.*"

His pleasant sketch of "the good peaceable man" and of the troubled and troubling man is equally graphic. First a general principle : "Keep thyself in peace, and then thou shalt be able to bring others to peace. The peaceable man does more good than"—we shall hardly suspect what is coming— "than *one that is very learned.*" The ironical flavour of this is pleasant—especially the "more" good—for he means, perhaps;

that the learned man does little or none.   The passionate man
—that is, the troubling, fussing man—"turns even good to evil,
and *readily believes evil,*" the one comes from the other.   On the
other hand, the "good peaceable man turns all things unto good.
Further, being in perfect peace, he has no suspicions ; while he
that is discontented and disturbed" is "agitated by various
suspicions ; he hath neither rest himself, nor suffers others to
rest. . . . He considers what others ought to do, and neglects
that which he is bound to do himself."

I have already quoted one or two eloquent, almost inspired,
passages.   Indeed it will be noted that wherever the topic is
grand and ennobling, he ever rises with it.   Thus urging his
favourite theme of the incompatibility between the world and
the service of our Saviour, he breaks into this fine, even
dramatic, burst: "Give, therefore, a dwelling-place to Christ,
and refuse entrance to all beside.   When thou hast Christ *thou
art rich,* and He is sufficient for thee.   He will provide for thee,
and *be thy faithful procurator* in all things : so that thou needst
not trust in men. . . . Why standest thou looking about thee
here, since this is not thy place of rest, . . . all things pass
and thou too along with them.   See thou cleave not to them,
lest thou be ensnared and perish.   Let thy thoughts be with
the Most High. . . . Rest in the Passion of Christ.   If thou
devoutly betake thyself to the precious Wounds of Jesus, . . .
thou wilt not care much for being slighted by man.   Christ was
willing to suffer and be despised, and darest thou complain of
aught?   Christ had enemies and detractors, *and wouldst thou
have all to be thy friends and benefactors.* . . . Endure with
Christ and for Christ, if thou wouldst reign with Christ."   These
burning, genuine words, must stir the hearts of the coldest.

Here is a comforting, reassuring, almost alluring passage :
" I am sufficient," our Saviour is supposed to say, " to recom-
pense thee beyond all bounds and measures. It is not long
thou hast to labour here. . . . Wait a little and thou shalt see
a speedy end of suffering. The hour cometh when all labour
and suffering shall be no more. All is little and short which
passeth away with time. Mind what thou art about, labour
faithfully : I will be thy reward. Write, read, sing, lament,
keep silence, bear adversities manfully, *eternal life is worth all
these, and greater combats*. And it will not be day or night,
such as it is at present, but light everlasting, infinite brightness,
steadfast peace, and safe repose."

This is beautiful language. The topics are put in the fairest
and most telling light, and there is an almost pathetic melody
in the words. And he concludes with a sort of " clincher,"
" *It is no small matter to lose or gain the Kingdom of God.*"

The value of these speculations lies in this: that they represent
a tone of mind which must be cultivated and reached before
anything really practical can be done. It is clearly the sensible
logical attitude, and contrasts with the ordinary illogical one,
which is that it is a sort of catastrophe or calamity to withdraw
from the world. On the coming of some dangerous illness,
when we are confronted with the possibility of death, we by
constraint, as it were, accept the situation, and prepare ourselves
as it is called. Of course it is only a really holy person that
will carry these theories into action; but still it is only "common
sense " to cultivate this attitude, and it is *not* common
sense to suppose that any sudden *volte face* and change of
attitude at the end can suit the scheme of salvation. It is an
invaluable thing to see the full, proper bearing of the whole

arrangement, even though we are too weak to apply it in practice. One of the most striking features of the book is the engaging fashion in which we are invited and persuaded to save ourselves, and it is too often overlooked that our Saviour is eager and longing that we should do so, having parted with His own life to that end. Good-will, even along with feeble, halting purpose, is what He desires.

There is something almost naïve in the following out-pourings on the subject of distraction : " Pardon and mercifully forgive me," he prays, " as often as in my prayers, I think of ought else save Thee. For I truly confess that I am accustomed to be very much distracted. For many a time I am not there where I am bodily standing or sitting, but am there rather where my thoughts carry me. There am I where my thought is ; and there oftentimes are my thoughts where that which I love is. That most readily cometh to my mind which naturally delighteth me, or which through custom is pleasing to me. . . . For whatever things I love, of the same I love to speak and hear, and I carry home with me the images of such." A pleasing natural and confidential sketch of a distracted soul.

The forcible character of the following contrast is truly striking : " For some mere trifle or a slight promise, men will brave toil day and night. But, alas, for an unchangeable good, for an inestimable reward, for the highest honour and never-ending glory, they are loath to undergo a little fatigue. Blush, then, thou slothful, querulous servant, that they are actually more ready to labour for death than thou for life. *They rejoice more in vanity than thou in the truth.* Sometimes, indeed, they are disappointed of their hopes ; but My promise deceiveth no man, nor sendeth away empty him that trusteth in Me. What I have promised I will give ; what I have said, I will make good ; if only a man continue to the end faithful in My love."

His reflections on the Blessed Sacrament in the fourth Book have a marked practical spirit and originality. Thus he alludes to the ardent faith of devout communicants, and the extraordinary prodig.es of exertion which this faith has produced, as "demonstrative existing argument of Thy sacred Presence." Sacrifices, sufferings, martyrdom, accepted with an eagerness all but miraculous, can only be accounted for by the consciousness of the Divine substance being thus communicated. This is a very striking thought. Again he suggests : "If this Most Holy Sacrament were celebrated in one place only, and consecrated by only one priest in the world, with how great desire, thinkest thou, would men be affected towards that place, that they might see the Divine Mysteries celebrated ? "

Here again he inculcates his favourite system of "instalments," which is so encouraging for the feeble. If you cannot obtain all, strive at least for a portion. Attempt something. "Who standing by a copious fire doth not derive therefrom some little heat ? Wherefore, if I may not draw out of the fulness of the fountain, nor drink to satiety, I will, at least, set my mouth to the opening of this heavenly pipe, so that I may draw thence some little drop to allay my thirst. And if as yet I cannot be all on fire, *I will still endeavour to follow after devotion*, and to prepare my heart, that so I may acquire some small spark of heavenly fire. And whatever is wanting to me, do Thou in Thy bounty and goodness supply for me, who hast vouchsafed to call all unto Thee, saying : 'Come to Me, you that labour,'" &c. "Endeavour to follow after devotion" is a useful counsel. Hesitation to approach the Holy Table on the ground of unworthiness, ill-preparedness, &c., often a snare, is dealt with in this plain, practical style. "Know that thou canst not satisfy for this preparation by the merit of any action of thine, even if thou shouldst prepare thyself for a whole year together, so as to think of nothing else. But it is of My mere goodness and grace that thou art suffered to come to My table, *as if a beggar should be invited to the banquet of a rich man. Do therefore what lieth in thee, and do it diligently*, not out of custom nor from necessity. . . . *I am He who hath invited thee. I have commanded it to be done; I will supply what is wanting to thee; come and receive Me.* . . . If thou hast not devotion . . . *persist in prayer, sigh and knock; thou hast need of Me, not I of thee.*"

In these few passages is found an invaluable guide in approaching the Holy Sacrament, and our relation to our Blessed Lord is put in the plainest way. I am tempted to quote here, from one of the old English versions, a portion of the opening chapter, which for its quaint simplicity and effectiveness will command admiration. After describing the subject-matter in this heading: "In what great reverence and fervent desyre we oughte to recyve our Lorde Jesu cryst," he quotes the opening passages from Scripture, "Come to Me," &c., and then goes on: "O my Lorde Jesus Chryst, eternal truth, these words beforesaid be Thy words. Albeit they have not been said in one self time, nor written in one self place, yet for that they be Thy words, I ought faithfully and agreeably to understand them. They be Thy words, and Thou hast professed them. And they be now mine, for Thou hast said them for my health. I will gladly receive them of Thy mouth, to the end they may be the better sown and planted in my herte. Thy words of so great pity, full of love, sweetness, and dilution, greatly exciteth me: but, Lord, my proper sins fereath and draweth back · my conscience, not pure to receive so great a mystery, draweth me sore abacke.   The swetness of Thy words incyteth and provoketh me, but the multitude of myne offences charge me very sore. . . . Angels and archangels honour Thee, and ryght wyse men drede Thee, and Thou sayst yet come all men unto Me.   But that Thou, Lord, haddest sayde it, who wolde believe it to be true?   But that Thou hadst commanded it, *who durste attempte to goe to it ?*"

Indeed, any one would "ride pleasantly enough," and be well founded in his religion, who has equipped himself with these sayings, selected at hap-hazard:

"No one is fit to comprehend heavenly things who hath not resigned himself to suffer adversities for Christ.

"Unless a man be disengaged from all things created, he cannot freely attend to things Divine.

"My sentence standeth sure: 'Unless a man renounce all he cannot be My disciple.'

"Be resigned to My good pleasure, and thou shalt suffer no loss.

"Leave curiosities alone.

"Sooner or later thou must be separated from all, whether thou wilt or no.

"Thou wilt never be devout unless thou pass over in silence other men's concerns, and look especially to thyself.

"Leave vain things to vain people.

"Inconstancy of mind and little confidence in God is the beginning of all evil temptations.

"Thou canst not be satisfied with any temporal goods, because thou wast not created for the enjoyment of such things.

"He that clingeth to the creature, shall fall with its falling."

And this above all, which contains "the philosophy" of the whole:

"*He whose taste discerneth all things as they are, and not as they are said, or accounted to be, is a truly wise man.*"

This is the basis of all spirituality. It is certain that at the last moment the vision will suddenly clear; and it would be a priceless gift to see now as we shall see then, but, as "the Bard" so finely puts it, it is a difficult thing, so long as "this muddy vesture of decay doth grossly close us up." But, as our author says, "Woe to them that know not their own misery"—one of his most significant, well charged passages. For he does not merely mean the sinner, the careless, the pleasure-seeker, the denyer, but those who do not think—who "see things as they are said, or accounted to be, but not as they *are*."

I must now conclude, and in concluding, I may say that in presenting these "odds and ends"—little scraps and patches without order or connection, picked out here and there—I have had only one object in view: to attract readers to this great book, by offering *bonnes bouches* and tit-bits, which shall tempt the reader to search out more for himself. I do not think that this has been attempted before. I am convinced that many of the striking things set forth in its pages have escaped even diligent readers, for, as I said at the beginning, so much is compressed into every passage, that it requires thought, study, and a slow consideration to see all that is contained therein. By the aid of such hints as I have been giving, we may at least.

to use our author's words, " set our mouths to the opening of
this heavenly pipe, so as to draw thence some little drops." And
so, with best wishes for further understanding of the *Imitation*,
I here take my leave ; repeating once more, that sublime,
inspiring passage, whose meaning seems to grow on us the
oftener it is repeated : " *Whatsoever is not God is nothing, and
ought to be accounted as nothing.*"

CPSIA information can be obtained
at www.ICGtesting.com
Printed in the USA
BVHW041143150622
639878BV00002B/4